ALTER CHRI

ALTER CHRISTUS

ST. PAUL SPEAKS TO PRIESTS

JOHN J. GILCHRIST

ave maria press   AMP   Notre Dame, Indiana

© 2005 by John J. Gilchrist

All rights reserved. No part of this book may be used or reproduced in any manner whatsoever except in the case of reprints in the context of reviews, without written permission from Ave Maria Press®, Inc., P.O. Box 428, Notre Dame, IN 46556.

www.avemariapress.com

International Standard Book Number: 1-59471-031-7

Cover and text design by John Carson

Cover photo © Corbis Images

Printed and bound in the United States of America.

Library of Congress Cataloging-in-Publication Data

Gilchrist, John J., 1929-
    Alter Christus : meditations for priests on the words of St. Paul / John J. Gilchrist.
        p. cm.
    ISBN 1-59471-031-7 (pbk.)
    1. Catholic Church--Clergy--Religious life. I. Title.

BX1912.G55 2005
242'.692--dc22

2004026402

Dedicated to the
great confraternity of the priesthood,
to those men
who mean so much
to so many.

With gratitude to Susan Hughes
for her support and endless hours of work,
and to all those who encouraged me along the way.

How Should I Read This Book?

The answer is, of course, any way that you want to read it. The book, I believe, can best be utilized as a stimulus to meditation. You may find that you agree with the concepts derived from the thoughts of Saint Paul and the commentary on his words. You may find something that jogs your memory of characters or situations that you have known or experienced. You may even disagree with what is written. All that is fine for you will have re-encountered the concepts of priestly life and now you will have compared it with your own ideas and attitudes.

So, I ask you, dear friend, to simply take the book as it is. Read just a page or two at a time. By the time you have finished, hopefully, you will feel affirmed. You will appreciate a little more your value and the gift you are to God's church.

Contents

My brothers in Christ,

There is nothing in the world quite like this priesthood that we share. Our common relationship arises from a variety of sources. Fundamentally, of course, we are privileged to share in the one great priesthood of Jesus Christ. We act in his person every time we approach an altar or perform a sacramental rite. We are his voice on the pulpit and in the role of teacher. We are all unique, of course, but this mysterious bond of ours underlies the very purpose of our lives, which is to make our Lord present upon the earth in his people.

Secondly, we have all at one point in our lives said "Yes" to this sacred calling. We have left all else to pursue the path of the apostles. We didn't offer something. We gave everything. We offered our lives to God.

Thirdly, we share a common training. The seminary experience may now be found in various forms, but the discipline of scholarship and the rigor of formation leaves all of us with a lived common experience. The memories of seminary life can never be erased.

Lastly, the priesthood, no matter what form it takes in parish, academia, or chancery, is no bed of roses. Yet there is no life that can be more rewarding or more filled with happiness than this ministry of service.

There are no finer, holier, or more generous men than those found among the Catholic clergy. We can share a thousand laughs. We even reminisce with joy at the funerals of priests. Most of us don't like to be too serious—except perhaps in support groups or in spiritual direction. But underneath it all, the priestly confraternity is real. It is almost palpable when priests gather. We sense the brotherhood.

Many years ago (1944) the Apostolic Delegate to the United States, Archbishop Amleto Cicognani put together a small book that he entitled *The Priest in the Epistles of Saint Paul*. It was a series of small excerpts from the Pauline Corpus—that is, from all of the letters attributed to Saint Paul.

He had divided these passages into various themes—for example, "Vocation," "The Nature of the Priesthood," and

"Priestly Life." Then he added his own brief meditations to each scripture reading. I personally found them very useful for examining this life that I was living. I never forgot the book over the years.

Now, almost fifty years later and after a life filled with experiences both good and bad, I have been emboldened to follow the lead of the good archbishop.

I have selected readings from Saint Paul's letters. I have added a host of thoughts from people who have written about the priesthood from the time of the Fathers of the Church until the twenty-first century. Finally, I have added my own brief reflections. They come from my life—not from books or from literary imagination.

I have been a parish priest, a teacher in a high school, a hospital chaplain, and in all sorts of apostolates. However, I would not want anyone to think that this priest who writes about the priesthood is any paragon of virtue. I have probably made more mistakes and generally fouled up as much as any priest alive. However, what I have been and what I have done may help other men, who are also not perfect images of holiness either, to persevere. After all, the great thing about Paul is that he was so human—just like me and you.

I guess the best thing that can be said of most of us is this. We are on the job. And we are still struggling to do God's work as best we can. Perhaps that's why the Lord loves us.

My hope is this: that sometime, somewhere in a stony little corner of the Lord's vineyard, a beleaguered brother will get a lift from reading this little book when things are tough. Perhaps the older guys will read and smile as they remember incidents in their own lives, and perhaps some younger men might gain an insight into the way things once were and how they have evolved.

So, my friends, this is my tribute to you in our common life as priests. Please accept my homage.

—John J. Gilchrist

PART ONE

You Are a Priest Forever. . . .

—Hebrews 5:6

A Call, Not a Profession: The Priest Is God's Man

1.

No one takes this honor upon himself but only when called by God, just as Aaron was. In the same way, it was not Christ who glorified himself in becoming high priest, but rather the one who said to him:

"You are my son;
this day I have begotten you." —Hebrews 5:4, 5

My brother,

While we are not like the original Calvinists, who believed in absolute predestination, nor Muslims who believe in Kismet (fate), yet is it not awesome to consider the words of Jeremiah, the prophet:

"Before I formed you in the womb I knew you.
before you were born I dedicated you,
a prophet to the nations I appointed you"
(Jer. 1:5)

It is not by some sheer coincidence, nor accident of history, nor mere happenstance that you came to exist. From all eternity, it was appointed that you were to be born. Before you were conceived in the womb, God knew you. In biblical terms, that also signifies that God loved you.

The reality is this: The whole of creation was waiting for your moment to arrive. There never was, nor ever will be, another you. You have your own genetic makeup. Like your fingerprints, no one will ever duplicate your voice, your mannerisms, your smile—in effect, all that goes into your personality. Your talents, your emotional disposition, even your instincts, are unique.

You were born into a certain family, in a certain environment. Your experiences, both good and bad, are singularly yours. Your responses to life situations have emerged from your own natural instincts and personality.

Don't you see, brother, that our dear Lord designed you and crafted you? He has made you for a mission that no other person will ever accomplish. This is your time.

> Father, they are your gift to me. I wish that where I am they also may be with me, that they may see my glory that you gave me. . . . —John 17:24

> Whenever Divine Goodness chooses a man for some particular service, God bestows upon him all gifts necessary for the man and his office and richly adorns him. —St. Bernardine

> God has created me to do him some definite service. He has committed some work to me which he has not committed to another.
> —John Henry Cardinal Newman

> . . . Behold, I come to do your will, O God.
> —Hebrews 10:7

2.

Do not lay hands too readily on anyone, and do not share in another's sins. —1 Timothy 5:22

My brother,

See how Paul warns his fellow bishops about the care that must be taken in calling men to Holy Orders.

Just think about your own journey. You had to live in a seminary where you underwent a long period of formation. You were carefully examined to see if you had mastered all of the theological knowledge for the priesthood. You were part of a formation program that introduced you formally to the spiritual life. You were separated from the world and given time to grow and mature in the ways of ecclesiastical life.

On your part, you walked a rigorous road of discipline. On the other hand, you also knew that you were being closely scrutinized.

And so, my friend, you were not lightly chosen or easily ordained. Therefore, you should recognize your worth, your dignity, and the esteem in which you are held.

You were carefully prepared to follow in the footsteps of the Master. Never underestimate your calling—or your dignity.

In the seminary of the late 1940s, there were many veterans who had served in World War II. When these men eventually compared their life stories, they were surprised to find one common experience that each had undergone. It was the nagging idea of becoming a priest. It entered some minds during battle, others at discharge. The reaction of each man seemed to have been the same, "Who? Me?" And God's answer was, "Yes—you!"

And the transference from military training to seminary was an easy step for them. It involved a new discipline—but for Christ.

> It was not you who chose me, but I who chose you. . . .
> —John 15:16

> You are always and everywhere the bearers of your particular vocation. You are the bearers of the grace of Christ, the eternal priest, and the bearer of the charisms of the Good Shepherd. —Pope John Paul II

> I must not be a teacher of political science, of human knowledge. There are teachers galore of these subjects. I am a teacher of mercy and truth. —Pope John XXIII

3.

Consider your own calling, brothers. Not many of you were wise by human standards, not many were powerful, not many were of noble birth. Rather, God chose the foolish of the world to shame the wise, and God chose the weak of the world to shame the strong, and God chose the lowly and despised of the world, those who count for nothing, to reduce to nothing those who are something, so that no human being might boast before God. —1 Corinthians 1:26–29

My brother,

The world has changed so much since Vatican Council II, and the turbulence of the changes in our holy church, especially in the liturgy, has affected us all.

The Second Vatican Council made an "opening to the world." In doing so, the church began to take into account the emotional side of the human person. It began to be influenced by the discoveries in psychology and the social sciences. The church also became more aware of the human needs of the priesthood.

At the same time, the need for the priest to fulfill many roles in service to the faithful began to influence the ideal of the priesthood. Yes, a priest must be a professional man, a cultivated man, a theologian, and at times, a sociologist or a business person, but we are not doctors, lawyers, nor scholars. We are not primarily social workers, or middle managers in the great corporation called the "Roman Catholic Church."

Essentially, we are called to be "other Christs." Like Jesus, our vocation comes from God, and has as its primary function to serve God by serving his community. We are shepherds in a pilgrim church. We are meant to be guides for God's people. They look to us, not for the things of this visible world, but for the spiritual.

There are many accountants, doctors, lawyers, and scholars, but very, very few priests. Our Jesus asks us to make him present in word and sacrament. It is his presence that we bring into the world. To form Christ in others, that is our call.

If all the world's a stage, then, brother, this is your time on stage in the spotlight. There is no dress rehearsal. For all of us, our time to shine is here and now.

> They do not belong to the world any more than I belong to the world. —John 17:16

> There are too many priests who, without dishonoring their calling and character, take low views of the dignity of their mission. —Jacques Millet, S.J.

> It is not the institution or structures [of society] that the priest has to transform, but the people and they themselves will do the rest. —Frederico Suarez

---

4.

I am grateful to him who has strengthened me, Christ Jesus our Lord, because he considered me trustworthy in appointing me to the ministry. —1 Timothy 1:12

My brother,

Paul thanks God for having strengthened him and judged him to be faithful. The almighty Creator has already made a judgment about you. He inspired your soul and guided your path to the altar.

The Lord himself has given you a dignity that surpasses all others—he has drawn you into his band of apostles. He has called you by name. He has deputized you. You are nothing less than his vicar and representative before the people of God.

He has placed you in the ministry. You share a precious sacred place among the glorious company of the servants of Christ, his priests.

Your vocation perdures, and Jesus is with you all days—all days until the end of the world.

Like a wandering troubadour, the priest has a song to sing. Wherever he goes, Christ goes with him. God's love must be told. And the very life of the priest is, or should be, a hymn of love. Let your life be a paean of praise to God in the cacophony of this world's noise.

I am the vine, you are the branches. —John 15:5

For after all, is not the priest God's man?
—Jacques Millet, S.J.

The priest does not belong to himself, just as he does
not belong to his family, or friends, or even a particular
country. His very thoughts, will, and sentiments are not
his, but belong to Christ, his life. —Frederico Suarez

If the Lord should grant me a long life and the
opportunity of being a useful priest in his church, I
want it to be said of me, and I shall be prouder of this
than of any other title, that I was a priest of lively
simple faith. —Pope John XXIII

5.

He saved us and called us to a holy life, not according to our
works but according to his own design and the grace
bestowed on us in Christ Jesus before time began. . . .
—2 Timothy 1:9

My brother,
Do you realize what the Lord has done for you?

All of creation comes from God. Therefore, all of the universe reflects God's goodness; its very existence comes from
the Creator and subsists by a continuing act of the Creator's
will. "By the LORD's word the heavens were made . . ." (Ps 33:6).

All Christians have been elevated by a new birth to a share
in the divine life. ". . . You have had yourselves washed, you
were sanctified, you were justified in the name of the Lord
Jesus Christ" (1 Cor 6:11). Therefore, every Christian can say,
"yet I live, no longer I, but Christ lives in me" (Gal 2:20).

But you, my brother, have been drawn into a union with our
Lord that identifies with him. You are drawn not only into his
liturgical function as priest and offering. You are drawn into
some share in his holiness.

This holiness, my brother, is ontological. When the bishop laid his hands upon you, you were radically transformed. You were permanently drawn into a reality that is from God, and rests in God, and it is now God who operates through you.

> . . . I, the Lord, your God, who have set you apart from the other nations. —Leviticus 20:24

> Priestly consecration attains its full value by affecting the ontological transformation that fashions the person in the divine model. —Jean Galot, S.J.

> It is Jesus who lives and acts in the priest.
> —Jacques Millet, S.J.

> Every time I've come across a successful priest whom the people respect, he can be dumb, he can be sometimes socially inept, but if he has holiness . . . that man succeeds. —Archbishop Oscar Lipscomb

---

6.

Be eager to present yourself as acceptable to God, a workman who causes no disgrace, imparting the word of truth without deviation. —2 Timothy 2:15

My brother,

"Handling the word of truth properly" is no small task. Our scriptures are a pastiche of events, concepts, and ideals that arouse an enormous number of reactions. We can use the scriptures to inspire, to support, to give hope, to arouse love, and a hundred other worthy emotions. We can also utilize the words of God's book to create fear, to intimidate, to rouse shame, to incite to anger, and to induce a multitude of other negative feelings.

To make ourselves worthy of the gospel, we must always strive to move our congregation to a new vision—a vision of hope and love in Jesus Christ. Jesus was never "no," Jesus was always "yes." That means that Jesus was always positive with his people. He was only negative with those who lived false lives of pseudo-piety.

There is no need to berate God's people. Nor is there any gain in being negative in a church that Jesus made all positive, all optimistic, all hopeful.

There was one priest who had only one sermon—and he preached it every Sunday. It was about the evil of abortion. He ranted. He raved. He literally called down thunderbolts from the sky. He was consumed with a righteous fury.

The problem was that those who endured his wrath were the innocent. Those to whom he aimed his wrath were not in church. Secondly, this "Johnny One Note" deprived the people of the "good news" of Jesus.

Eventually, he left the priesthood.

> Moreover, we possess the prophetic message that is altogether reliable. You will do well to be attentive to it, as to a lamp shining in a dark place. . . . 2 Peter 1:19

> The habitual and normal character of the parish priest should be mild and compassionate.
> —Jacques Millet, S.J.

> The precious truth that sounded forth from the mouth of the Lord was written for our sakes, preserved for our sakes, and recited for our sakes —St. Augustine

> The priest's role is to "make sense of the mess."
> —Dean Hoge

7.

For the gifts and the call of God are irrevocable.
—Romans 11:29

My brother,

A call from God is not something that God gives and takes away. It is important that we remember that the "call" is from God. Our response must come from the depths of our being.

But even after we have said, "*Adsum,*" "Here I am," the ultimate and final proof of our vocation lies with the church. Our vocation is ratified, completed, and sealed by the imposition of the hands of the bishop. A sacred character was impressed upon your very being. You were given, in virtue of that character, power—power to consecrate the body and blood of Christ, the power to forgive and retain sins so that the faithful might be spiritually prepared to receive this great gift of the Eucharist.

And so, you are a priest forever.

In my time, a man was hit by a car. A bus happened to be there. The bus driver got off the bus and gave the dying man absolution. He had been an "active" priest. Now no longer active, he was nevertheless still a priest.

Brother, you are a priest. Nothing can ever change that—*In eternum*, forever.

> He made him perpetual in his office
> when he bestowed on him the priesthood of his
> people;
>   He established him in honor
> and crowned him with lofty majesty. . . . —Sirach 45:7

The priesthood is a call, not a career.
—Timothy Dolan

The object that priests strive for by their ministry and life is the procuring of the glory of God the Father in Christ.
—Decree on the Ministry and Life of Priests

The priesthood is the love of the heart of Jesus.
—The Curé of Ars

8.

But you, remain faithful to what you have learned and believed, because you know from whom you learned it, and that from infancy you have known [the] sacred scriptures, which are capable of giving you wisdom for salvation through faith in Christ Jesus. All scripture is inspired by God and is useful for teaching, for refutation, for correction, and for training in righteousness. . . . 2 Timothy 3:14-16

My brother,

Paul speaks to Timothy, but through Timothy, he addresses us.

Has not our entire training been formed by and wrapped in the scriptures? The scriptures are our tools, our instruments, our very mechanism for bringing Christ to life for our people.

How is it, then, that so many times we approach the pulpit to read the sacred word, and then we simply drop it and move on in our preaching to other topics? Brother, the people do not need to hear your life story. They do not yearn to hear your opinion on world events. They do not need sermons on money, or their shortcomings.

The people need to be fed twice at every liturgy—once by the word and once by the Holy Sacrament. Scripture is more than just useful. It is a necessity for spiritual life. Feed the flock!

He said in reply, "It is written:
'One does not live by bread alone,
  but by every word that comes forth
  from the mouth of God.'" —Matthew 4:4

If preachers and priests of God's word make so few conversions, it is because there is in them too much of human wisdom, and too little of divine fire.
—St. Teresa of Avila

A simple word from the gospel has more power over souls than all of the vehemence and all of the ingenuity of human eloquence. —Jacques-Benigne Bossuet

Unfortunate indeed is the teacher who preaches like a wise man, yet who lives like a fool. —Jacques Millet, S.J.

When you give a sermon, someone is going to sweat— either you in preparing it, or the people who have to listen to it. —Monsignor George Baker

If you are going to preach the gospel, at least read the thing first. —Father Jerome Murphy O'Connor, O.P.

9.

So you, my child, be strong in the grace that is in Christ Jesus. And what you heard from me through many witnesses entrust to faithful people who will have the ability to teach others as well. —2 Timothy 2:1, 2

My brother,

We are all links in a chain. What came from the apostles was handed on to us. We are those who will move God's church into the future. We hand over our treasure every day to those who will come after us.

No other church, no other institution on the face of God's earth, has a gift such as ours. Our scripture, our tradition, our deposit of faith, our saints, our history, and yes, even our sinners have all contributed to this great tapestry of history—the story of the one holy Catholic church.

So once in a while, my friend, if you are feeling inconsequential or even depressed, stop and see yourself. What the apostles were, you are now. What all of our spiritual ancestors did, you are now performing. You are the trustworthy steward caring for, and passing on, the gift of God to future generations.

And he replied, "Then every scribe who has been instructed in the kingdom of heaven is like the head of a household who brings from his storeroom both the new and the old." —Matthew 13:52

The Catholic priesthood possesses the most sublime and magnificent power on earth. They are depositaries of a great moral force that can move the world. —Jacques Millet, S.J.

The priest is a solitary figure fighting to keep a torch alight in an atmosphere capable of quenching every supernatural spark. —Frederico Suarez

The priesthood today means an understanding of the hard mission of the church, trying harder to make man see what he [man] really is. —Pope Paul VI

The priest can never be the servant of an ideology or a faction.
—The Priest and the Third Christian Millennium

THE ESSENCE:
TO OFFER SACRIFICE

10.

*Now every high priest is appointed to offer gifts and
sacrifices....* —Hebrews 8:3

My brother,
    How clean our priesthood is. There is no awful slaughter of
animals, no need to be covered with blood, no need to terminate
life or destroy food. Our altars are clean—almost antiseptic.
There is usually beauty all around us. There is the comforting
mumble of voices in prayer, almost like the sound of running
water. There are low lights, at times the odor of incense. There
can be music—a joyful song—or occasionally a plaintive
melody. There are flowers in season.
    We offer the gifts of bread and wine. Our sacrifice is invisi-
ble to the physical eye, yet all bespeaks of the hushed tone of
God's presence.
    My brother, appreciate what you do. Take time now and
then to rejoice in your holy environment. The liturgical sacrifices are easy and refreshing.
    The other sacrifices of your daily life are more difficult. The
holy Mass will strengthen you for the offering of your life to
God.
    There are priests in our area who offer a twelve-minute Mass
on weekdays and a seventeen-minute Mass on Sundays. The
people—at least a certain portion of them—seem to love it.
What does it say about our worship?

Let my prayer be incense before you;
    my uplifted hands an evening sacrifice.
—Psalms 141:2

Our whole being should be seized with fear. The whole world should tremble and heaven rejoice when Christ the Son of the Living God is present on the altar in the hands of the priest. What wonderful majesty! What stupendous condescension! O sublime humility! That the Lord of the whole universe would humble himself like this and hide under the form of a little bread for our salvation. —St. Francis of Assisi

The priest, holding the host, has all the treasures of God in his hands. —Jacques Millet, S.J.

If a priest is not on his guard, he may become accustomed even to the most sacred things and get into a routine, an almost mechanical and absent-minded way of doing things whose very nature demands the greatest attention and all the refinement of which he is capable. —Frederico Suarez

11.

Every high priest is taken from among men and made their representative before God, to offer gifts and sacrifices for sins. He is able to deal patiently with the ignorant and erring, for he himself is beset by weakness and so, for this reason, must make sin offerings for himself as well as for the people. —Hebrews 5:1–3

My brother,

There is no need to lecture you or any priest about his personal weakness.

Every one of us has been given the Christian ideal as a model. I doubt that any priest who has ever lived has been able to even approximate that model—because the model is Christ himself.

Monsignor John Fahy, who was pastor of St. John's in Orange, New Jersey, was, during World War II, a chaplain for Theresa Neumann, the stigmatic who lived in Konnersreuth, Germany. John said that large numbers of American soldiers came to visit her. Whenever a priest was among them, even if his insignia were covered, Theresa invariably looked at him and said, "Good day, Father." She knew because the priest was consecrated to Christ and bore his seal.

Almost every priest carries within himself those hopes and dreams of a holy life that were formed in the seminary. And almost every priest secretly in his heart laments that he has fallen short of the ideal. In some cases, we have not only fallen short, we have self-destructed spiritually.

But, brother, look around. See all the sinners. Their burden is your burden. Their weaknesses are your weaknesses. So continue to make those sin offerings through the holy Mass—for yourself, for your people.

At each liturgy, at the beginning, we become *one* with our people—one in our confession of sin. Consider, my friend, we are one in sin with the best and the worst. That thought can be devastating and consoling at the same time.

> I will give you a new heart and place a new spirit within you, taking from your bodies your stony hearts and giving you natural hearts. —Ezekiel 36:26

> Even the most lamentable downfall, which through human frailty is possible to a priest, can never blot out from his soul the priestly character. —Pope Pius XI

> Fix your hope on heaven, and then be certain that help will always be yours. —Blessed Agnes of Prague

> I did not ask for praises, which make me tremble; what I know of myself is enough to confound me. —Cardinal Frederico (in *The Betrothed*)

12.

*Then he says, "Behold, I come to do your will." He takes
away the first to establish the second. By this "will," we have
been consecrated through the offering of the body of Jesus
Christ once for all.* —Hebrews 10:9–10

My brother,

In Jeremiah 31:31, God said that he would make a "new
covenant with the house of Israel and the house of Judah." We
are now partakers in that new covenant.

Consider that, since the year 70 A.D., there has been no
Temple in which to offer, in a bloody manner, bulls and goats
and sheep. But now, wherever you set up your altar, whether
in a great cathedral, a quiet parish church, or even in a field,
you are attended by the invisible hosts of heaven. Your liturgy
resounds through the vaults of heaven. Your whispered words
are power, for they enable God to come to man, and man to go
to God in a way that commands all of creation to attend.

You proclaim this "Blood of the New and Everlasting
Covenant." The word "covenant" or *brit* in Hebrew signifies
that which is "carved" in everlasting rock. Oh, my brother, in a
world where priests are so few, where the Masses are so many,
how difficult it is to recognize what we say we are handling, to
maintain the proper reverence.

The Jewish people were a holy people, a priestly people.
They were faithful in their role of preparing the world for our
dear Savior. Now, it is our time. We must not rush or carelessly offer the Holy Sacrifice. The very angels of God are present.

. . . This is my blood of the covenant, which will be
shed for many.—Mark 14:24

The celebrant must intend to do three things: to
worship God with adoration, commemorate the death
of Christ, and to aid the church. —Jacques Millet, S.J.

The powers bestowed upon the priests to be exercised in the name of Christ are divine powers. Thus, the priest emerges as the man of God, the man in whom God acts with special power. —Jean Galot, S.J.

The Eucharistic action is the very heartbeat of the congregation of the faithful over which the priest presides. —Decree on the Ministry and Life of Priests

13.

. . . *but he with an oath, through the one who said to him:*
"The Lord has sworn, and he will not repent:
'You are a priest forever'"—

to that same degree has Jesus [also] become the guarantee of an [even] better covenant. Those priests were many because they were prevented by death from remaining in office, but he, because he remains forever, has a priesthood that does not pass away. Therefore, he is always able to save those who approach God through him, since he lives forever to make intercession for them.

It was fitting that we should have such a high priest: holy, innocent, undefiled, separated from sinners, higher than the heavens. —Hebrews 7:21–26

My brother,

It is well that you understand that you are only sharing in a priesthood that pre-exists, that perdures, and that will last in this world until the final day of the universe. It was Jesus to whom God spoke when he said, "The LORD has sworn and will not waver: 'Like Melchizedek you are a priest forever'" (Ps 110:4).

There was but one priest, one victim, one altar of the cross. It was and is a unique sacrifice. Never before could humankind do anything that could remotely begin to, in any way, atone to the Creator for the disobedience of man's ingratitude to our God. All of creation, from the first "Big Bang" until today, has obediently followed God's plan. Only the human race has deviated from its original course.

Now, in a sense, the cross stands eternally before the Lord Jesus who, living in his priests, re-presents himself to the Father from moment to moment, age to age. You, unworthy though you are, have been privileged to enter into the very economy of salvation.

Each day, our poor offering is elevated to a newer and higher plane. Our feeble hands offer bread and wine. Invisibly, yet really, Jesus becomes present. "From the rising of the sun to its setting" (Ps 113:3), as the High Priest offers himself to the Father and we are his instruments. Truly, this is an awesome thought.

> . . . "This is my body, which will be given for you; do this in memory of me." —Luke 22:19

> The ministerial priest, by the sacred power he enjoys, models and rules the priestly people. Acting in the person of Christ, he brings about the Eucharistic sacrifice and offers it to God in the name of all the people. —Lumen Gentium

> Priests, the fate of the world rests with you. Be holy at the altar and the world will be saved.
> —Jacques Millet, S.J.

> The priest is a living and transparent image of Christ the priest —Decree on the Ministry and Life of Priests

14.

Therefore, brothers, since through the blood of Jesus we have confidence of entrance into the sanctuary by the new and living way he opened for us through the veil, that is, his flesh, and since we have "a great priest over the house of God," let us approach with a sincere heart and in absolute trust, with our hearts sprinkled clean from an evil conscience and our bodies washed in pure water. Let us hold unwaveringly to our confession that gives us hope, for he who made the promise is trustworthy. We must consider how to rouse one another to love and good works. —Hebrews 10:19–24

My brother,

I know that you have sensed the loneliness of the priest at the altar.

Consider the ministry of the word. There in the synagogue of the faithful, all pray together. We hear the word spoken or sung by lectors, cantor, or choir. We speak to the congregation. We maintain a union that is consoling and human.

But after the offertory of the gifts, you find yourself in a new position. You are the mouth and the hands of the congregation as you offer the bread and wine to the Lord. You speak in the plural, for you are truly representing God's family. It is "we," "us," and "our," and never "I," "me," or "mine." You lift the community in spirit to join the very cherubim and seraphim in singing the *Trisagion,* "Holy, Holy, Holy, Lord God of power and might."

Then, you move into the Eucharistic prayer. You assume the person of Christ to transform bread and wine into the body and blood of Christ.

At that mysterious moment, you are wrapped in divine action. No one but you—no words but yours—and suddenly Christ is present.

To their God they [the priests] shall be sacred, and not profane his name; since they offer up the oblations of the Lord, the food of their God, they must be holy. —Leviticus 21:6

When I see the priest standing erect before the altar, I
see the angels silent and in admiration.
—Jacques Millet, S.J.

The sacramental character of orders elevates the human
creature to the level of the divine activity of Christ.
—Gustav Thils

The whole life of the Christian reaches its summit when
it is offered in union with the priest's sacrifice at the
Eucharistic liturgy through the priest.
—Raymond A. Tartre, S.S.S.

15.

*For I received from the Lord what I also handed on to you,
that the Lord Jesus, on the night he was handed over, took
bread, and, after he had given thanks, broke it and said, "This
is my body that is for you. Do this in remembrance of me."*
—1 Corinthians 11:23-24

My brother,

After the consecration, all of the community is riveted upon
one place. The altar is truly an altar, for upon it rests the Lord
of the Universe, offering himself anew to the Father.

It took Saint Padre Pio two full hours to celebrate the holy
liturgy because, when he offered the liturgy, the sacred words
of consecration were no mere sounds, no human speech. He
was wrapped into the mystery of the cross.

Cardinal Ratzinger has made the observation that, "Without
the cross, the Eucharist would always be empty ritual. Without
the Eucharist, the cross would be just a cruel profane event."

Poor humans that we are, our minds are like skittish horses
that tend to go off in many directions. Yet, what lies before us
at Mass transcends all physical reality. The "economy of salvation" is at our fingertips.

Yet all of us have known the experience of beginning the
eucharistic prayer—and suddenly we have become distracted—
and we find ourselves at the Our Father wondering how we

got there. At times saying Mass can almost be like saying the Rosary. Why not switch eucharistic prayers now and then? It helps to focus our attention.

> ... "This cup is the new covenant in my blood, which will be shed for you." —Luke 22:20

> The priestly character is character in the highest degree, in its most complete realization, the most intensive participation in the priesthood of Christ.
> —Jean Galot, S.J.

> The sacrifice of the Lord is not complete as far as our sanctification is concerned unless our offerings correspond to His passion. —St. Cyprian

> The Eucharistic Sacrifice is the center and root of the whole priestly life.
> —Decree on the Ministry and Life of Priests

16.

For as often as you eat this bread and drink the cup, you proclaim the death of the Lord until he comes.

Therefore whoever eats the bread or drinks the cup of the Lord unworthily will have to answer for the body and blood of the Lord. A person should examine himself, and so eat the bread and drink the cup. For anyone who eats and drinks without discerning the body, eats and drinks judgment on himself.
—1 Corinthians 11:26–29

My brother,

These sentences are enough to frighten a thinking man away from the Eucharist. Who of us is pure enough to receive the body and blood of the Lord?

Yet, in the seventeenth century, Jansenism used precisely this passage to scare the faithful from communion with the Lord. And the effect of this heresy lasted into the twentieth century. There were and are many people who would not receive unless they had gone to confession each time they were to go to communion.

The devotion to the Sacred Heart was the antidote to Jansenism. Our Lord had to make huge promises to induce people to receive holy communion once a month.

Now, of course, we have swung the other way. It is discouraging to see people coming to communion in such a casual way. It is almost as if they were saying, "Oh, I'll have one of those" (meaning the host) as if they were buying a cookie at the bakery.

Brother, celebrate your Mass with devotion. Receive the Eucharist with fervor. Spend a few seconds with the Lord after communion and before giving out the sacrament. The people will see in your love for Christ the example they need to approach the Eucharist with devotion.

> For the bread of God is that which comes down from heaven and gives life to the world.—John 6:33

> What the priest takes up is not what he replaces on the altar. The immortal flesh of Christ is set down upon it. What was natural food has become spiritual food. What was the momentary refreshment of man has been made the eternal and unfailing nourishment of the angels.
> —Stephen, Bishop of Autun

> O singular and admirable liberality when the giver comes as the gift and is himself completely given with the gift. —Pope Urban IV

17.

The cup of blessing that we bless, is it not a participation in the blood of Christ? The bread that we break, is it not a participation in the body of Christ? —1 Corinthians 10:16

My brother,

A little while ago, a poll showed that less than half of all Catholics actually believe in the real presence of Christ in the Blessed Sacrament. How to account for this lack of faith is a problem, but not our only problem.

Our need is to preach Christ and him crucified. Our need is to enhance our own love of Christ under the sacred species. Some priests have time to spend an hour each day with the Lord. Some priests are so totally occupied that all they can do is make a short visit.

But, brothers, the heart and soul of our ministry is the Eucharist. Without Eucharistic devotion, we are hardly Catholic priests. We are ignoring the very reason for our being.

So why not detour your path each day through your church or chapel? Even a "Hello, Lord," and a quick genuflection speaks volumes about your faith and your love.

Eucharistic devotion and faith can only return to the faithful if the priests are filled with zeal and love for the Christ who lies hidden in the sacrament.

For what great nation is there that has gods so close to it as the Lord, our God, is to us whenever we call upon him? —Deuteronomy 4:7

Alas, how little is all that I do! How short the time I spend in preparing for holy communion! I am seldom wholly recollected and very seldom indeed free from distraction. Yet, surely, with the presence of your life-giving Godhead, no unbecoming thought should arise and no creature possess my heart, for I am about to receive as a guest, not an angel, but the very Lord of angels. —Thomas à Kempis

The noblest sacrament, therefore, is that wherein the body is really present. The Eucharist crowns all other sacraments; and though all are instruments of grace, and his life and death work through them all, it is there that the sacramental causality reaches its height.
—St. Thomas Aquinas

Your Love has hidden itself in silence, so that my love can reveal itself in faith. —Karl Rahner, S.J.

18.

For we are God's co-workers . . . . —1 Corinthians 3:9

My brother,

This is an awesome thought. If Paul is correct, then we are not just laborers in the Lord's vineyard; God himself is our partner. He is invisibly present in our apostolate. That which we do in a physical and visible way is accompanied by God's assistance in an invisible and spiritual manner.

Too many priests feel that the apostolate depends entirely upon them. Therefore, they judge the success or failure of their life in terms of human measurement. Thus, if my parish grows and flourishes, I am apt to take great pleasure in my managerial abilities. If it struggles and falters, I feel guilty. It is the same with any other enterprise.

Friend, God does not judge by our standards. He sees things in eternal light. Success and failure are not to be seen in any other than God's judgment. Sometimes in God's plan, you win by losing. Look at the cross.

During the post-World War II years in the United States, there was a huge migration of Catholics to the suburbs. Replacing them were people of color pouring into the cities.

Parishes that were once thriving Catholic communities suddenly witnessed entire congregations disappear. One pastor said, "I am so weary of saying 'goodbye.'"

Many priests stayed in the cities. They struggled to keep their parishes alive. Worries of every sort plagued their lives.

These were heroes. Yet, in all truth, failure seemed to be their fate.

God's ways are not our ways, nor does God judge things as we do.

. . . And behold, I am with you always, until the end of the age. —Matthew 28:20

It is in our weakness that the power of God is manifested through the Paraclete, the Holy Spirit. —Jean Vanier

Like his master, the priest is called to carry out the work of redemption and there is no other path of salvation, no other way by which people can be saved, but by the way of the cross. —Frederico Suarez

A good skipper can steer a boat through many a storm, and does not cease to be a good skipper if he cannot save the boat. —Thomas Vernon Moore, M.D., Carthusian

19.

So we are ambassadors for Christ, as if God were appealing through us. —2 Corinthians 5:20

My brother,

Every ambassador needs credentials. Every ambassador needs a briefcase. Your baptism made you a prophet of God, a priest of the most high as a member of the church, and a member of the royal family of God.

Your ordination made you much more, not only in degree, but also in the very nature of your office. You are the "official" spokesperson for Christ and his church for the faithful and the world. You are the mouthpiece of God, the official who prays in the name of the community, the priest who offers the sacrifice of Christ's body and blood. You are an essential stone in the structure of this mystical church of God.

Walk tall, brother. Remember whom you represent and for whom you speak. However, beware of putting on airs, or being artificial.

There was a priest among us who was a "name-dropper." He had "been with" the governor. He "knew" the senators. He was a familiar figure in the secular world. Everyone saw him clearly except himself. He became a figure of ridicule.

> By this is my Father glorified, that you bear much fruit and become my disciples. —John 15:8

> The priesthood is the mysterious ladder of Jacob on top of which God rested and the priests are the angels who go up and down, continuously keeping an uninterrupted communication between earth and heaven. —Jacques Millet, S.J.

> The sacerdotal office of the priests is conferred by that special sacrament through which priests, by the anointing of the Holy Spirit, are marked with a sacred character and so configured to Christ, the Priest, that they can act in the person of Christ, the Head. —Roman Pontifical, Priestly Ordination

> For what is the summit of the priestly apostolate other than this: Wherever the church lives to gather around the altar, the people joined together in the bonds of faith, reborn in baptism and cleansed from their sins? —Pope John Paul II

> The fact is that the more I speak about myself, the more virtue I lose; vanity squirts out of every word, even from those which seem most innocent. —Pope John XXIII

20.

Thus should one regard us: as servants of Christ and stewards of the mysteries of God. —1 Corinthians 4:1

My brother,

The mysteries we touch are so holy that, by comparison, they make our hands unclean. The High Priest of the Second Temple period prepared to enter the Holy of Holies on Yom Kippur by fasting, abstaining from any sexual activity, and by washing his body until it was immaculate. The clothes he wore for this priestly function were worn only once a year. And finally, he was kept under guard for twenty-four hours prior to his sacrificial duty.

You, my brother, enter day after day into the mystery of the holy liturgy. You are dealing with the sacred every day. You are, in this, God's co-worker (1 Cor 3:9).

You are, regardless of your weakness or failings, the Man of God (1 Tm 6:11).

So stop and consider who and what you are.

Wherever you create the mystery, God is present.

If you ask anything of me in my name, I will do it.
—John 14:14

In the character impressed by priestly ordination there resides a profound and indelible principle that engenders assimilation to Christ. —Jean Galot, S.J.

O priest, to you is entrusted the vast treasure of the blood of Jesus Christ. You alone have the power to offer up the august sacrifice which enriches the church, gives joy to heaven, and brings refreshment to the souls in purgatory. —Jacques Millet, S.J.

The priest must be a man of God, but this will serve him little if his social intercourse is by a vulgarity that insults the human personality and dignity of his fellow men. —Raymond A. Tartre, S.S.S.

I can only stand helpless and feeble before the ultimate
mystery of myself, a mystery which lies buried,
immovable and unapproachable, in depths beyond the
reach of my ordinary freedom. —Karl Rahner, S.J.

21.

*I am writing you this not to shame you, but to admonish you
as my beloved children. Even if you should have countless
guides to Christ, yet you do not have many fathers, for I
became your father in Christ Jesus through the gospel.*
—1 Corinthians 4:14–15

My brother,
   Listen to the above. Non-Catholic Christians years ago took
a great deal of pleasure in reproaching priests because the
faithful called us "Father." Remember how they quoted Jesus,
"Call no one on earth your father" (Mt 23:9).
   Well, listen to Saint Paul. He knew the words of Jesus, and he
completely understood that his words brought people to a new
life in Christ. He was completely happy to be called "Father."
   You too deserve the title. Carry it proudly. By word and
sacrament, a priest will bring many to supernatural life over
the years.
   But to bear the title with honor, you must live up to the title
and all that is implied. You must be a father to your family. We
are God's representatives in the spiritual world.
   The priest was at the bedside of his terribly ill friend. They
had been classmates in a small public grammar school and
high school. They had known each other for almost sixty years.
   As he finished anointing his friend, the priest was startled to
hear him say, "Thank you, Father."
   As the priest left the hospital, he felt uneasy. What an enormous honor! The office of priest had subsumed the man. The
priest felt humbled. Christ had been at the bedside in his person.

As you sent me into the world, so I sent them into the world. And I consecrate myself for them, so that they also may be consecrated in truth. —John 17:18–19

Priests therefore constitute a section of the people of God to whom the church has entrusted an extremely important and exceptionally delicate task, namely to transform the world by transforming men.
—Frederico Suarez

The priest is truly the "father" to his faithful.
—Gustav Thils

22.

. . . apostles of the churches, the glory of Christ.
—2 Corinthians 8:23

My brother,
   Saint Paul is speaking of Titus and his other brethren. He calls them apostles for the churches.
   You are an apostle for the church. By your ordination and your mission, you have been sent to share in the work of the ministry. You are the apostle of Christ. You are a co-worker with the bishop.
   Paul, Titus, and the others had their day. Now, it is your day. This time, this age, this generation is yours to evangelize, to catechize, to sanctify, and to serve. Look around you. All the people you see are yours. They are your mission.
   This is much more difficult today than in centuries gone by. Our people are more educated, far more knowledgeable, and more influenced by the culture of the modern world. They are more resistant to the truly spiritual.
   But do the best you can and you will be known as, and will truly be the glory of Christ—his light shining on the Gentiles.

Go, therefore, and make disciples of all nations. . . .
—Matthew 28:19

The diocesan priests are *"apostoloi,"* sent into the world
to be the "salt of the earth," the leaven in the dough, the
good odor of Christ. —Gustav Thils

The apostle is a "contemplative in action."
—Jerome Nadal

The apostolic spirit is to outside activities what the soul
is to the body. —Gustav Thils

The priest in his own distinctive way leads the people
into this mystery of God in Jesus and calls down the
purifying fire of forgiveness for the missionary
transformation of our whole universe.
—George A. Aschenbrenner, S.J.

23.

*The latter act out of love, aware that I am here for the defense
of the gospel. . . .* —Philippians 1:16

My brother,

Saint Paul is speaking in his imprisonment. He says that his
situation has worked out to further the gospel. His imprisonment for Christ was well-known throughout the praetorium,
and to others as well.

Christians, Jews, Romans, and Gentiles were all aware, not
only of his suffering, but also of Christ for whom he was suffering. "What difference does it make," says Paul, "as long as
in every way, whether in pretense or in truth, Christ is being
proclaimed?" (Phil 1:18).

The scandal of a jail cell only enhanced Paul's message of
Christ for the world. My friend, have you ever considered that
all of the circumstances of your life contribute to the preaching
of the gospel? No matter where you are, no matter what your
physical condition, no matter what your position, no matter
what trials beset you or honors glorify you, it can all be for the
glory of God. Every day is a new opportunity to preach the
wonders of God. Every day, without words, you preach.

The priest was called to jury duty. There was no way out. So, armed with a book and paperwork to pass the time while waiting to be called, the priest settled himself each morning in the large room provided for potential jurors. There he sat each day for two full weeks.

But the priest never read his book, nor did any paperwork. One by one, people came to sit beside him. He did more counseling and heard more confessions than he would have in his parish. Oh yes, he was finally called, but the case was dismissed. A priest is a priest anywhere.

> My son, when you come to serve the Lord,
> prepare yourself for trials. —Sirach 2:1

> The leader of all priests is Jesus . . . poor, suffering, and humble. —Jacques Millet, S.J.

> If a man measures the value of his work by its immediate and apparent fruits, he will quickly lose heart. If he lives in accord with his morning sacrifice, he will spend himself in his ministry for Christ, even though his efforts lead nowhere.
> —Eugene Boylan, O.C.R.

24.

> *. . . our authority, which the Lord gave for building you up and not for tearing you down. . . .* —2 Corinthians 10:8

My brother,

You have been given power. It lies in your authority as ambassador of Christ. It lies in your power to give the sacraments.

This power has been given to you as it was given to Saint Paul, not for breaking down the mystical body of Christ by crushing its people, but for nourishing them, fostering them, and strengthening them. Your power is granted you to be used wisely, not for harm but for good.

Harsh words and rejection have no place in the priesthood. Yes, some people are difficult. But some are too weak to bear

your admonitions. Some are not worthy of the sacraments—at
least, not yet—but they are all in a precarious position. One
rejection too many will drive them away from Christ, perhaps
forever.

So, be gentle, my friend. A little humor will help. Jesus had
to go with the flow when it came to the weak and the ignorant.
So must you.

In a city parish, the words of Jesus, "the poor you will
always have with you," are literally true. Those "poor" are not
simply people in poverty. There are the psychologically poor—
the mentally ill, the emotionally poor, who cannot handle their
lives; the morally poor—the hustlers, the con artists, the handouts; and the spiritually poor, who cannot distinguish their
right hand from their left.

Without a sense of humor, the priest will himself need a psychiatrist. The "poor" can literally drive you to drink unless you
see them as Jesus did—as his friends.

> . . . I have made you a light to the Gentiles, that you
> may be an instrument of salvation to the ends of the
> earth. —Acts 13:47

> So that the priestly ministry may be truly sanctifying, it
> must truly be an act of theological charity. —Gustav Thils

> Guide souls more by praying and beseeching than
> commanding. —St. Bernard

> There are priests, pious priests, whose conduct gives you
> a cold chill. —Jacques Millet, S.J.

> A saint is the incarnation of the gospel and of the highest
> principles of Christian spirituality.
> —Thomas Vernon Moore, M.D., Carthusian

CONSECRATED LIFE:
THE PRIEST AS TOTAL GIVER

25.

If you will give these instructions to the brothers, you will be a good minister of Christ Jesus, nourished on the words of the faith and of the sound teaching you have followed. Avoid profane and silly myths. Train yourself for devotion, for, while physical training is of limited value, devotion is valuable in every respect, since it holds a promise of life both for the present and for the future. —1 Timothy 4:6–8

My brother,

The bar is so high. Our human abilities are so inadequate.

The life set out before us is nothing less than the imitation of Christ: " . . . yet I live, no longer I, but Christ lives in me" (Gal 2:20).

Were we hermits or monks, all of our lives could be of prayer and fasting. Great sins and moral faults would be much easier to withstand. Prayer and study could fill our lives.

But ours is no easy path. There are trials and temptations of every form waiting to distract us, worry us, disturb us, or tempt us. "Is not man's life on earth a drudgery?" asks Job (Jb 7:1).

"For I do not do the good I want, but I do the evil I do not want. . . . Miserable one that I am! Who will deliver me from this mortal body?" cried out Saint Paul (Rom 7:19, 24).

We have consolations, brother. The love of Christ drives us. "In him who strengthens me, I can do all things." (Phil 4:13). I can fight the good fight. Holiness will be mine. "As for me, to be near God is my good . . ." (Ps 73:28).

. . . your hearts will rejoice, and no one will take your joy
away from you. —John 16:22

O, the loftiness of the clerical dignity, which gives up the
whole world that it may possess God alone, and in turn be
possessed by Him. —St. Jerome

What the Holy Spirit has done for martyrs, He will surely
do for priests. —Aloysius Biskupek, S.V.D.

Holiness and growth in union with God always involve
the full human person alive in the present concrete
situation of the world. —George A. Aschenbrenner, S.J.

Very few of God's saints are canonized.
—Thomas Vernon Moore, M.D., Carthusian

26.

*Let no one have contempt for your youth, but set an example
for those who believe, in speech, conduct, love, faith, and
purity. Until I arrive, attend to the reading, exhortation, and
teaching. Do not neglect the gift you have, which was
conferred on you through the prophetic word with the
imposition of hands of the presbyterate. Be diligent in these
matters, be absorbed in them, so that your progress may be
evident to everyone. Attend to yourself and to your teaching;
persevere in both tasks, for by doing so you will save both
yourself and those who listen to you.* —1 Timothy 4:12–16

My brother,
   You are not your own. You are Christ's. By your ordination,
you entered a new role. You were changed, transformed in
your essence, so that you might act *in persona Christi*. You have
become his person, his servant, and his representative. You are
one of the "Stewards," one of the guardians and protectors of
the mysteries of salvation.
   "Now it is of course required of stewards that they be found
trustworthy" (1 Cor 4:2).

At times, it is difficult to remember whom we represent. If we celebrate the holy liturgy, in a church that has so few people that we feel alone, if we recite words that we have spoken so many times before, and especially if we feel exhausted, then, my brother, it is time to reflect on what we do. At this moment, in this place, even though no other human realizes what is truly happening, Jesus, by your stewardship, is able to intercede in time, on this earth, before the Father.

"Do this in memory of me" actually means, "Make me present again." And you, my brother, are a link in a chain that extends from the cross to eternity. Though no human realizes what is happening, all the hosts of heaven stand in adoration at your side.

> "For from the rising of the sun, even to
>   its setting,
>   my name is great among the nations. . . ."
> —Malachi 1:11
>
> You are "apostles of the churches, the glory of Christ".
> —2 Corinthians 8:23
>
> . . . I have made you a light to the Gentiles, that you may be an instrument of salvation to the ends of the earth. —Acts 13:47
>
> The priest does not belong to himself, just as he does not belong to his family, or friends, or even to a particular country. His very thought, will, sentiments are not his; they belong to Christ, his Life.
> —Pope Pius XII
>
> The character of the priesthood remains engraved on a priest's soul and no power on earth can remove it.
> —Aloysius Biskupek, S.V.D.

The deepest reason for the distinctive role of the priest in the eucharist lies in the fact that only God can offer worthy sacrifice to God. The Christian God is so transcendent to the world, so holy, that no act of human religion is adequate in His presence.
—Robert Sokolowski

27.

Through him [then] let us continually offer God a sacrifice of praise, that is, the fruit of lips that confess his name. Do not neglect to do good and to share what you have; God is pleased by sacrifices of that kind. —Hebrews 13:15–16

My brother,

When Israel had a temple, each day the smoke of holocausts rose into the sky. But after the temple was destroyed, Israel was forced to offer to the Lord a sacrifice of prayer and good works.

Each day, we pray silently at the altar, before reading the gospel, "Almighty God, cleanse my heart and my lips that I might worthily proclaim your gospel."

We are a bit like Isaiah, who, having had a glimpse of heaven cried out, "Woe is me, I am doomed! For I am a man of unclean lips, living among a people of unclean lips" (Is 6:5). Isaiah was purified by a burning coal that was placed on his mouth by an angel.

Yet we, poor creatures that we are, live in a society that delights in irreverent, impure, and even blasphemous speech. How can the people of God hear and honor the word of God if it emanates from a mouth that praises God on the altar, but dishonors him by words that dishonor the priesthood in day-to-day pursuits.

Is it not fitting that we ask God each day to cleanse our minds, and our hearts, and our lips from all that is vain, evil, or distracting?

> Let my prayer be incense before you;
> my uplifted hands an evening sacrifice.
> —Psalms 141:2

Father, I am unworthy to appear before you; but I have absolute confidence in the Holy Humanity of Your only Son. United with His Divinity, I dare to present myself before you, and united with the Word, I sing your praise. —Dom Marmion

Whoever offers sacrifice should participate in the sacrifice, because the external sacrifice which is offered is the sign of the interior sacrifice. —St. Thomas Aquinas

And although it doesn't surprise me that men should recognize you when you come to meet them in your only begotten Son, or in the chaste water of baptism, or in the silent form of the host, or in the words of Scripture, so simple and yet so profound, still I find it all but incredible that you desire to come into Your Kingdom in the hearts of men through me. How can men possibly recognize you in me? —Karl Rahner, S.J.

28.

For, although we are in the flesh, we do not battle according to the flesh, for the weapons of our battle are not of flesh but are enormously powerful, capable of destroying fortresses.
—2 Corinthians 10:3–4

My brother,

This translation does not carry the full implication of the word of Saint Paul. He says that we do not wage war according to the "flesh" (*sarx*). Our weapons are not of the flesh (*sarkika*) either. We have at our disposal rather the power (*dunamis*) of God.

This separates us completely from the world, its values, and its objectives. In our life, we have as our model the crucified Jesus. In our world, so often we win, as Jesus did, by losing.

In the priesthood, so many of our hopes, desires, and dreams can be shattered so easily. The love we seek from parishioners does not come. Projects that begin with high hopes fizzle, or end in ruin.

We can also find that we are wounded by those in our own house, by those whom we trusted, our fellow priests. It is then the time to conquer our own flesh, our pride, our resentment, by imploring God's gift of equanimity.

We have overcome by fixing our gaze on the crucified. We relate to the psalmist who said,

> If an enemy had reviled me,
>   that I could bear;
> If my foe had viewed me with contempt,
>   from that I could hide.
> But it was you, my other self,
>   my comrade and friend,
> You, whose company I enjoyed,
>   at whose side I walked
>   in procession in the house of God (Ps 55:13–15).

We are one, as priests, even though we are many by reason of our individual differences and the bewildering confusion of our wayward human passions. We are one because we are stamped with the indelible character of priestly ordination which unites us to Christ, and through Christ to one another.
—Cardinal Richard Cushing

The life of the priest is a life hid with Christ in God.
—Jacques Millet, S.J.

Each of us is what he is in God's eyes.
—Frederico Suarez

One must live not only for God but from God.
—Cardinal Mercier

Self-command comes by earnest practice. It is never a
gift of nature.
—Thomas Vernon Moore, M.D., Carthusian

29.

. . . serve the living and true God and to await his Son from
heaven, whom he raised from [the] dead, Jesus, who delivers
us from the coming wrath. —1 Thessalonians 1:9–10

My brother,

At all holy liturgies we recite the memorial acclamation,
which is also the foundation stone of our belief: "Christ has
died, Christ is risen, Christ will come again."

The early church had an intense belief in the imminent
return of the Lord. Surely, it is reflected in the words of Jesus,
when he said, " Amen, I say to you, there are some standing
here who will not taste death until they see that the kingdom
of God has come in power" (Mk 9:1).

And also at his trial, when he said,

". . . and 'you will see the Son of Man
seated at the right hand of the Power
and coming with the clouds of heaven.'"
(Mk 14:62).

But we are now fully aware that the providence of God is not
a short range operation. Ours may actually be the infant
church. There is a long way to go in the fulfillment of God's
design for the universe.

You and I have our role here and now. This is our time in the
economy of salvation. We must not become discouraged when
things seem to go against God's church. We Catholics may
even become yet a smaller minority in the world of men.

But then remember! You, my brother, are part of the seed, the
leaven that will grow and permeate the world, until that day
when there will be but one cry from pole to pole. Praise to the
Divine Heart that wrought our salvation.

... but take courage, I have conquered the world.
—John 16:33

Being a priest, I am a man of God, charged with
whatever pertains to His honor and glory.
—Jacques Millet, S.J.

The world sees that the priest places at the very center
of existence, something which, even if the world
recognizes it, it will only tolerate at the periphery
God and His reality. —Joseph Sellmair

With an eternity of freedom, and a fullness that will
always stagger our earthbound consciousness, God will
be God, far beyond any effort of ours.
—George A. Aschenbrenner, S.J.

30.

Let love be sincere; hate what is evil, hold on to what is good;
love one another with mutual affection; anticipate one
another in showing honor. Do not grow slack in zeal, be
fervent in spirit, serve the Lord. Rejoice in hope, endure in
affliction, persevere in prayer. Contribute to the needs of the
holy ones, exercise hospitality. Bless those who persecute
[you], bless and do not curse them. Rejoice with those who
rejoice, weep with those who weep. Have the same regard for
one another; do not be haughty but associate with the lowly;
do not be wise in your own estimation. —Romans 12:9–16

My brother,
    How fickle our human nature is. We so easily change. We
honor or love someone today. Tomorrow, we can forget or
ignore them.
    That is where honor lies. The just man does not waver. Like
Saint Paul, who declared that his word was not "Yes" one
minute and "No" the next. No, Paul was like Jesus, the Son of
God, who was not alternately "Yes" and "No." He was never
anything but "Yes" (cf. 2 Cor 1:19).

How easy it is to love "those who love you" (Lk 6:32). Among our parishioners, among our acquaintances, even among our family, how many times we love some, honor some, and ignore others.

To be honest, in dealing with people, we are not lying on a bed of rose petals. There are too many thorns, too many prickly characters, too many who want something, too many who are just too cheap, mean, or ornery to love.

But, in today's world, one of the greatest insults in human relations is to ignore phone calls, or to refuse to return phone calls. There are, of course, some who are, in fact, a nuisance. But when we will not speak to people, or we leave them in limbo, waiting for a response, then perhaps we should question our fidelity to duty.

Ordering the secretary, or the housekeeper, to tell all callers (except the bishop or the chancery) that you are "out" may be acceptable once in a while. But a priest who is always "out" is certainly not "there" to the people.

> Woe to you when all speak well of you,
>   for their ancestors treated the false
>   prophets in this way. —Luke 6:26

> One temptation that can slip in [the life of a priest] is professionalism, the tendency to make the service of God and souls into a business. Such a priest changes from a man with a mission into a paid religious official. —Frederico Suarez

> Our Lord's plan for each priest is a personal partnership—We—Jesus and I. —Aloysius Biskupek, S.V.D.

> See to it that nothing in the church deteriorates through your negligence. —Roman Pontifical

> Persevere in prayer, being watchful in it with thanksgiving. . . . —Colossians 4:2

31.

Pray without ceasing. In all circumstances give thanks, for this is the will of God for you in Christ Jesus.
—1 Thessalonians 5:17–18

My brother,

Prayer is, in a sense, our business. We were ordained precisely to offer "spiritual sacrifices acceptable to God" (1 Pt 2:5).

Our people come to us. Again and again, they ask us to pray for them or their intentions. They rightly feel that while all people have a vocation, a job to do in life, our work is to stand before God on their behalf.

As priests, we go to God. We are a "pontifex," a bridge builder between the Almighty and his creation.

It is only in virtue of our ordination that we have this special position. Many people are more holy than we. Many are personally more deserving.

But when we offer Mass, say our office, or offer our own prayers, we do not go before God on our own. It is Jesus Christ, the only and true High Priest, who renders our prayers worthy and effective. When we pray, it is the voice of Jesus that the Father hears.

So never be discouraged, my friend. Yes, your sins and faults may be many. But when you stand at the altar, when you pray the office, when you are the minister of the sacraments, Christ prays in you and with you.

> To you, O God of my fathers,
>   I give thanks and praise,
>   because you have given me wisdom and power.
> —Daniel 2:23

If the priest's soul is over worldly, he will see the breviary as of no practical purpose whatsoever.
—Frederico Suarez

The mysteries you celebrate on the altar are not cold, official acts; they are the heartbeat of the redeemer.
—Aloysius Biskupek, S.V.D.

If the priest is to be capable of doing God's work, he must belong to God with his whole being. Grasped by God in his whole being, he can radiate and communicate with God by everything that he is.
—Jean Galot, S.J.

When you get busy, what is the first thing that seems to go? It's prayer. —Anonymous

So often I consider my prayer as just a job I have to do, a duty to be performed. I "get it out of the way" and then relax, glad to have it behind me. When I'm at prayer, I'm at my "duty," instead of being with You.
—Karl Rahner, S.J.

32.

. . . Keep yourself pure. —1 Timothy 5:22

My brother,

Purity of heart can mean many things.

In today's world, because the media is so saturated with sexual situations and inferences, we think of purity only in physical terms. The entire culture and our environment is pervaded with libidinous references.

However, innocence and purity imply more for the psalmist and the sage. It implies simplicity, honesty, integrity, straightforward behavior that is completely reflective of the integral physical person.

We must not let the sixth and ninth commandments so occupy our thoughts and moral life that they obscure all else. Duplicity and dishonesty, greed and ambition, spite and jealousy, meanness and egoism—all are destructive. Pure hands do what a pure heart commands. Be honest with yourself! Be honest, friend!

The clean of hand and pure of heart. . . .
—Psalms 24:4

By requiring that life be celibate, consecration gains
control over one's heart and activity. —Jean Galot, S.J.

Those who proclaim and teach the word of God must
zealously renounce marriage in order to dedicate
themselves to the performance of loftier ideals.
—Origen, *Homily on Leviticus 6:6*

Celibacy posits a vivid sign of that future world which
is already present through faith and charity and in
which the children of the resurrection will neither
marry nor take wives.
—Decree on the Ministry and Life of Priests

Celibacy is rooted in a priest's religious experience of
the awesome, inviting attractiveness of God's love.
—George A. Aschenbrenner, S.J.

Conscious willing is found even in infants, but
consciously accepted obligation is the sign of a mature
man. —Karl Rahner, S.J.

33.

*Immorality or any impurity or greed must not even be
mentioned among you, as is fitting among holy ones, no
obscenity or silly or suggestive talk, which is out of place, but
instead, thanksgiving.* —Ephesians 5:3–4

My brother,
Note the words, "Let them not even be mentioned among
you." Oh priest. Your holiness forbids even talking of such
things. It is not as if you were an unconsecrated person in secular life.
You were consecrated in baptism, and filled with the Spirit at
confirmation. Ah, but at ordination, you put on Christ. He is
you. You are him.

So, the problem is this. Any defilement, any sin, is not your defilement, your sin alone. It has wider ramifications for Christ's body, the church. Your innate special state must be protected and guarded because you are Christ's and Christ is God's.

All that is of the flesh wars against not just your spirit, but against you—and the Christ you bear within you.

Most of us have been present at this scenario. It is a public function, perhaps a banquet or communion breakfast. A priest is called upon to say a few words. He decides to tell a joke. It may or may not be funny. At the punch line, there is an uncomfortable silence or a few laughs. The joke was off-color, or just inappropriate.

What may work for a lay person can be an embarrassment for the priest. The people expect better from us.

> We have given up everything and followed you.
> —Matthew 19:27

> Celibacy enables the priest to better actualize his consecration to Christ with undivided love.
> —Jean Galot, S.J.

> The heart of the priest, in order that it may be available for service [to the people of God] must be free. Celibacy is a sign of freedom that exists for service.
> —Pope John Paul II

> Priests, as ministers of the sacred ministries, especially in the sacrifice of the Mass, act in a special way in the person of Christ who gave himself as a victim to sanctify men. And in this way, they are invited to imitate what they handle; so that as they celebrate the mystery of the Lord's death, they may take care to mortify their members from vices and concupiscences.
> —Roman Pontifical, Priestly Ordination

34.

*But put on the Lord Jesus Christ, and make no provision for
the desires of the flesh.* —Romans 13:14

My brother,

In the pre-Vatican Council II world, the above message could
only refer to the allurements of the flesh. There was not much
opportunity for a priest to sin in other ways.

Yes, alcohol could be a terrible attraction for some. Cigarettes
were very inexpensive. Some priests gambled, and some gambled heavily.

But basically, there was little opportunity for profligate living. Rectory and religious life was circumscribed with rules
and customs. Priests had very little money. They lived on sub-
sistence wages and their daily needs were met.

Now, however, much has changed. A priest in the modern
world is a middle-class person with access to a good salary,
benefits, and even luxuries.

When Saint Paul spoke of the desires of the flesh, he could
not have envisioned expensive cars, houses, trips, jewelry, and
in short, all the benefits of today's "good life." Jesus was poor
and free. Are you free, my friend?

There was a priest who came to America after World War II.
He stayed in the Archdiocese and was allowed to work in a
university. He had nothing but contempt for the diocesan
priests around him. "They are," he said, "too rich and worldly.
They know nothing of holiness."

Ten years later, there was a small piece in the *Newark Evening
News*. Our friend from Italy had suffered an auto accident on
South Orange Avenue in Newark. He had crashed his Cadillac
into another car. Interesting!

> Go, sell what you have, and give to [the] poor and you
> will have treasure in heaven; then come, follow me.
> —Mark 10:21

The worldly man lacks the perspective of eternity.
—Gustav Thils

The character impressed on the soul by the priestly ordination bespeaks a new being which in turn calls for a new way of life to be the expression of that character. It demands a total consecration of a man's nature.
—Jean Galot, S.J.

The more we indulge in soft living and pampered bodies, the more rebellious we will become against the spirit. —St. Rita of Cascia

35.

Since we have these promises, beloved, let us cleanse ourselves from every defilement of flesh and spirit, making holiness perfect in the fear of God. —2 Corinthians 7:1

My brother,

There are as many different priesthood lifestyles as there are priests. All of us are so very different. No two voices, no two fingerprints, no two DNA patterns, no two personalities are the same. You are special. As the old song states, "There will never, ever be another you."

Therefore, your struggle to be holy, your personal heritage, talent, interest, and psychological makeup, taken all together, create your one distinct life.

Yes, we share a common priesthood in Jesus Christ. But you shape and mold your vocation in your own style. You must strive, therefore, to fulfill your dream, your course according to God's plan, in your own particular manner.

Your struggles will also be your own. Others can advise and even help. But you alone are the steersman in your own vessel of life.

The pre-Vatican Council II seminary had many hidden faults. One was this. They preached humility, and simplicity, and especially holiness of life. At the same time, they set up a system that created sheep and goats. The brighter fellows were often pitted against each other. The prize was an education in Rome, Louvain, or Innsbruck. The winners were on a career track to ecclesiastical honors. The rest were destined to be "parish priests." The hidden psychological scars of that system hurt many, and later, many of those damaged by the system left the priesthood.

> My soul, be at rest in God alone,
>   from whom comes my hope. —Psalms 62:6

> We are nothing of ourselves, but by clinging to God, we have the means to make something of ourselves.
> —Jacques Millet, S.J.

> The soul for which the priest must answer is, before any other, his own. —Frederico Suarez

> Why do you follow your own flesh? Turn around and let your flesh follow you. —Saint Augustine

> Honors and distinctions, even in the ecclesiastical world, are vanity of vanities . . . anyone who has lived in the midst of these stupidities, as I did in Rome, and in the first ten years of my priesthood, may well insist that they deserve no better name. —Pope John XXIII

36.

I urge you therefore, brothers, by the mercies of God, to offer your bodies as a living sacrifice, holy and pleasing to God, your spiritual worship. Do not conform yourselves to this age but be transformed by the renewal of your mind, that you may discern what is the will of God, what is good and pleasing and perfect. —Romans 12:1-2

My brother,
    This age is really not so different from other ages. Human nature does not change. As the lyrics of the song from the movie *Casablanca* say, "It's still the same old story, a fight for love and glory, a case of do or die."

In our case, the offer of our lives to God in the priesthood happens to also involve the consecration of our lives in a celibate state. Our consecration means essentially that the priest is a lone man—not necessarily a lonely man. We meet people. We love people. We serve people. Then we move on. We have in this temporal world no abiding dwelling place. We have no permanent family.

It is the way of the itinerant Christ we follow. Never lonely, but always in certain ways, quite alone.

A normal priest is a normal man. If he does not find himself attracted to certain people, he would not be human.

It is also interesting that, among the saints, we find so many male-female relationships—Francis and Clare, Vincent de Paul and Louise de Marillac, Francis de Sales and Jane Frances de Chantal.

As the Jesuits used to say, "watch beginnings." It is easy to love someone—and unfortunately easy to "fall in love." Guard your heart. But cherish good people and holy relationships.

. . . for I, the Lord, am sacred, I, who have set you apart from the other nations to be my own. —Leviticus 20:26

A priest is obliged by his position to live in a world permeated by an atmosphere of excessive liberty and sensuality, often morally alone and seldom fully understood. —Pope John XXIII

The priest is *segregatus a mundo*; any attempt to find his happiness in world associations will result in disappointment. —Aloysius Biskupek, S.V.D.

The priest is not a man of the world. —Gustav Thils

The priest must be a man of God, the one who belongs to God and makes people think of God.
—Pope John Paul II

37.

If then you were raised with Christ, seek what is above, where Christ is seated at the right hand of God. Think of what is above, not of what is on earth. For you have died, and your life is hidden with Christ in God. —Colossians 3:1-3

My brother,

A priest ideally lives a bivalent life. On one hand, he is mortal. He walks among men, bearing all the burden of human weakness. He is a man among others. The inner man is obligated, each and every day, to encounter an outer world. No day is easy, because there is no day without some stress. It is just the way it is.

Yet, on the other hand, the priest is asked to walk, mentally and spiritually, on the lonely path to perfection. He is asked to see all things in the light of God's providence. He is asked to make invisible reality visible to those under his care.

Yes, my brother, you are asked to live your hidden life in Christ. But you, priest, have not died, except to the world. Your hidden life is the strength that enables Christ to operate in and through you.

During the 1940s, a priest whose job took him from diocese to diocese by train began to notice that, in so many towns through which he passed, especially in the Midwest, there would be a single church steeple mounted by a cross. As he passed through the farm belt and prairies, he would see that cross on a lonely hill.

Later, he would say, "As I went through those places, I said a prayer, because I knew that there was a lone priest in that church. He was, in my eyes, a hero. Christ was present because he was there."

I am the vine, you are the branches. —John 15:5

As Jesus Christ and the church are not two Christs, but one Christ, so the Eternal Priest and all priests born in time are not a multitude of priests, but one priest.
—Jacques Millet, S.J.

A priest cannot perform a single act of ministry on his own. He is one with Christ. He is the branch on the vine. —Eugene Boylan, O.C.R.

Holiness is no longer defined by participation in that otherworldly realm ritually produced in our own sanctuaries. —Dean Hoge

38.

. . . always carrying about in the body the dying of Jesus, so that the life of Jesus may also be manifested in our body
—2 Corinthians 4:10

My brother,

These words were so meaningful when we began our spiritual journey. Serving the Lord was a joy. We ran along the way of perfection. Every day was a new day of opportunity—a new day to meet challenges and to break down obstacles that barred our way to a more productive ministry.

But as we get older, there can be no doubt that we begin to feel the weight of our own mortality. Our step is not as quick as it once was. We tire more quickly. The problems of everyday service can seem a greater burden. In short, time slows us down.

But, as Paul says, while the outer man may decay, the inner man can continue to grow and flourish. Wisdom does come with age. We see things more clearly. We have a better perspective.

My friend, trust me. When the day comes that your own bishop looks like a youngster, you are ready to ascend to a new philosophical level. The body may not be as vigorous, but the mind sees clearly. The life and wisdom of Jesus is ready to be revealed in your life.

Senior priests should be looked upon as a treasury of experience. They are, so often, able not only to say, "been there, done that," but they also know what consequences come from having been there and having done that.

How becoming to the gray-haired is judgment,
    and a knowledge of counsel to those on in years!
—Sirach 25:4

You are always and everywhere the bearers of your
particular vocation. You are the bearers of the likeness
of Christ, the eternal priest, and the bearers of the
charism of the good shepherd. —Pope John Paul II

The life of the clergy is the book of the laity.
—Gustav Thils

You can't put an old head on young shoulders.
—Bishop John J. Dougherty

39.

*But our citizenship is in heaven, and from it we also await a
savior, the Lord Jesus Christ.* —Philippians 3:20

My brother,
    We may well have our citizenship in heaven. But the hard
reality is that, for now, we live in the hard world.
    More than that, while we may at times sense the reality of
the spiritual dimension, for the vast majority of our days, we
live, move, and have our being in the world of the senses.
What we see, hear, smell, taste, and touch is more immediate
than the heavenly Jerusalem.
    So, yes, we eagerly await the coming of the Lord. But until
that "Great Day of the *Parousia*," we must struggle constantly
to keep the spiritual dimension alive in our hearts and minds.
    The contact with God is prayer—conscious prayer, prayer
that rises from the heart and reaches for the infinite.
    My friend, the one thing that people expect in us is that we
be—each of us—a pontifex, a bridge builder to God. For many,
it is your words, your ministry, and your life that makes the
invisible visible—the unseen Creator seen with the eyes of
faith.

There was a delightful Baptist minister in Newark who would say, "Yes, my true home is in heaven. But right now, I'm not homesick."

However, every so often, a priest needs to speak about heaven—and eternity. There is an unspoken fear that haunts our society. It is the fear of death. Christ has conquered sin and death. We need to offer a vision of what will be. Yes, our people need reassurance.

> Your priests will be clothed with justice;
>   your faithful will shout for joy. —Psalms 132:9

> The example of the pastor is the book and gospel of most Christians. —Jacques Millet, S.J.

> A certain heavenly mindedness befits the priest as one who must know, speak of, and breathe into others the love of heavenly things. —Pope Pius X

40.

> *. . . God of all encouragement, who encourages us in our every affliction, so that we may be able to encourage those who are in any affliction with the encouragement with which we ourselves are encouraged by God. For as Christ's sufferings overflow to us, so through Christ does our encouragement also overflow.* —2 Corinthians 1:3-5

My brother,

Freely have you received. Freely give! There is absolutely no doubt that the servant of Christ has much to suffer in the course of his ministry. There are many trials to endure.

Yet, in the priestly vocation, the consolations of the spirit are always available. The holy Mass itself is our daily bulwark against trial and tribulation of the spirit.

So, since God is so good to us, we must impart our own blessing and consolation on the weak, the disturbed, those in pain, and especially those who are lost in sorrow.

Conversely, since we have also known times of desolation, we can also empathize with those who feel similarly abandoned by God. Your touch, in times of dark and doubt, are a Godsend to the faithful. My friend, you are a spiritual healer of immense power. Recognize your gift, and freely bestow it on the faithful. That is what priesthood is all about.

More and more, the rituals of death are being changed. Wakes are short. Funeral Masses are omitted. People are almost afraid to grieve.

Brother, if your presence was ever needed, it is needed at the time of death. Your very presence is an assurance of God's love and afterlife. If possible, never skip a wake. Prepare the homily for the Mass of the Resurrection. If possible, go to the cemetery.

Believe it or not, the faithful find in your very presence the assurance of eternal life.

Come after me, and I will make you fishers of men.
—Matthew 4:19

The faithful can expect from him who sets forth the doctrine of life, warm words from a priestly heart, carrying a profound conviction, a burning faith, and supported by a life which does not contradict the values which are being preached. —Gustav Thils

The spirit of love and service is an ontological exigency; it is rooted in what a priest is. —Jean Galot, S.J.

Although priests owe service to everybody, the poor and the weaker ones have been committed to their care in a special way.
—Decree on the Ministry and Life of Priests

41.

. . . guard what has been entrusted to you. Avoid profane
babbling and the absurdities of so-called knowledge.
—1 Timothy 6:20

My brother,

Saint James says, with great wisdom, "If anyone does not fall short in speech, he is a perfect man, able to bridle his whole body also" (Jas 3:2).

How many times have we embarrassed ourselves by speaking in an unwise manner? How many faults have come from our ungoverned words?

There is a proverb that a drunken man's words are a sober man's thoughts. Therefore, my friend, if you wish to be without fault in the spoken word, it is necessary to cleanse the heart, for from the fullness of the heart, the mouth speaks.

It is difficult, if not impossible, for a priest to be a respected priest if he is a foolish priest. Yet, be not discouraged if you fail. Time can bring a pure heart and an honest tongue. Silence, in the meantime, can be golden.

During the Vietnam War, there were two parishes in neighboring towns. In one, the priest—a peace activist—raged and ranted against the war and the American government. He did this almost every Sunday.

Down the street, in the next town, a priest thundered and exploded with patriotism every Sunday. He was a veteran of World War II—a super-patriot.

Meanwhile, the little ethnic parish nearby filled up each Sunday with folks who just wanted to receive the Lord in word and sacrament. If you can't find peace at Mass, where can you find it?

For from the fullness of the heart the mouth speaks.
—Matthew 12:34

The people are quick to perceive whether a priest
speaks from his heart or only from his lips.
—Cardinal Manning

There are priests who utter a volubility of utterance . . .
wherewith they strike the ears and gain their hearers'
admiration, but give them no lesson to carry home.
—Pope Benedict XV

42.

Therefore, brothers, stand firm and hold fast to the traditions
that you were taught, either by an oral statement or by a
letter of ours. —2 Thessalonians 2:15

My brother,

Constancy is a day-by-day virtue. To remain faithful and
constantly revisit and reinforce our faith is a necessity.

One of the most astounding aspects of our faith is the one
single fact that it has endured. The scripture is as alive and as
relevant today as it was when it was written.

We twenty-first century Catholics are so fortunate. Thanks to
wonderful scholars (scripture men, archaeologists, anthropolo-
gists, linguists, and others) we have a far more perfect understanding of our heritage than the most brilliant theologians of
the past. Our seminaries have given us a treasure—a broad
view of the history of our faith. Not one essential truth of our
faith has been shaken loose; the seamless garment of our belief
remains.

Give your people the best, my friend. You are a Renaissance
man. Let your people live in this new age.

The seminary was a place of turmoil long before Vatican
Council II. In one seminary, the professor of dogma refused to
speak to the professor of scripture. In his class, the enemies of
the church (liberal Protestant theologians) were in the foot-
notes at the bottom of the page. They were there to be refuted.
In the scripture class, some of the same theologians were presented as the guiding lights of exegesis. How fortunate are the
young men of today. They have the benefit of the struggles and
pains of theological and scriptural progress.

The Advocate, the Holy Spirit, that the Father will send in my name—he will teach you everything and remind you of all that [I] told you. —John 14:26

The ecclesiastical doctor must teach both by his life and his doctrine, for doctrine without life renders him arrogant, while life without doctrine renders him useless. —St. Gregory the Great

The Church itself is being engulfed and shaken by the tidal wave of change, for however much men may be committed to the Church, they are deeply affected by the climate of the world. They run the risk of becoming confused, bewildered, and charmed, and this is a state of affairs that strikes at the very roots of the Church. It drives many people to adopt the most outlandish views. They imagine that the Church should abdicate its proper role and adopt an entirely new and unprecedented mode of existence.
—Pope Paul VI, *Ecclesiam Suam*

43.

Endure your trials as "discipline"; God treats you as sons.
For what "son" is there whom his father does not discipline?
—Hebrews 12:7

My brother,

When we were young, we were treated as children. We were praised or rebuked as our conduct invited. The purpose was to guide and instruct us to see clearly not only right from wrong, but to recognize danger and seek the good.

Within us, there are forces—often seemingly out of our control. Catholics call it concupiscence, the inordinate desire of our own spirit and body. The Jews call it *"yetzer ha ra—yetzer ha tov,"* the pull to evil balanced by pull toward the good.

Now that we are older, we are left to our own devices as we make our way to eternity. But we are not alone. The infinite creator has a total interest in us. While we do not create the problems that we sometimes encounter, neither can we "blame" God for the troubles and difficulties of our lives. They are a natural part of living.

Where then is God? He is deep within our being—operating through the power of the spirit. The grace and strength we need lies deep within. Each new crisis brings us to a conscious response.

Our inner spirit can be torn in two directions. But sometimes everything is on the line. Surrender and we lose. Fight the good fight and we are strengthened in the power. We must become disciplined—trained in holiness.

> Asceticism is by no means a form of hostility to nature, a mere negation of something, but something positive because it involves refusing harmful things.
> —Frederico Suarez

> Learn through your charge to command your passions so that the enemy might find nothing in your conduct to claim as his own.
> —Roman Pontifical, Order of Exorcist

> To learn to stand with Jesus, sometimes in pleasure, at other times in pain, is the wisdom of a person planted more and more in the ground of God's love.
> —George A. Aschenbrenner, S.J.

> Are you only the distant horizon surrounding the world of our deeds and sufferings, the horizon which, no matter where we roam, is always just as far away?
> —Karl Rahner, S.J.

44.

For I am not ashamed of the gospel. It is the power of God for the salvation of everyone who believes: for Jew first, and then Greek. —Romans 1:16

My brother,
It is difficult to speak God's word in a world where humans have abandoned the moral power of belief in God.

"A prophet," said Jesus, "is not without honor except in his native place and in his own house" (Mt 13:57). All of the prophets of God were rejected in one way or another by the Israelites. Even Moses had resistance from a complaining and stiff-necked people.

Why then should you complain, O priest of God, when the forces of the world conspire against your message and even against you? How can you be a Christ figure without the cross? Why should you be upset when even your own ignore your message? You may be a voice calling in the wilderness, but you are God's voice.

Tell them what they want to hear and they will love you. Tell them what they don't want to hear, and many of them will want to "kill the messenger."

Without cost you have received; without cost you are to give. —Matthew 10:8

The men to whom I have been sent are of Your choosing, Lord, not mine. . . . For the most part, they won't even listen to me when I come in Your name. They have absolutely no desire for Your grace and Your truth, the gifts You have given me to bring to them. And yet I must keep pounding on their doors again and again, like an unwanted but persistent peddler.
—Karl Rahner, S.J.

Our brethren in the faith, and unbelievers too, expect us to always be able to show them "the things that no eye has seen and no ear has heard"; to be real witnesses to it, to be dispensers of grace, to be servants of the word of God. —Pope John Paul II

How do they [newly ordained priests] understand how to cope with either being deified or vilified by those they serve? —Mrs. Marti R. Jewell

Experience shows that priests who try to be more useful by doing what they think will make them more popular end up by being neither supernaturally useful nor humanly popular. —Thomas J. McGovern

45.

Do not rebuke an older man, but appeal to him as a father.
Treat younger men as brothers. . . . —1 Timothy 5:1

My brother,

The fraternity of the priesthood is the most binding and most noble of all callings. We may not be, as the popular song cries, "One in the Spirit, One in the Lord," at least, in our opinions. There is a Latin saying, *Omne agens agit secundum naturam suam.* That means there are different strokes for different folks. That is why they make chocolate and vanilla ice cream.

We are all different. Yet each of us has his own virtues. Each has his own faults.

Younger priests must give some ground to older priests. They have borne the burden of the day's heat. Older priests must not just endure, but even rejoice in, the enthusiasms, and yes, sometimes even the foolishness of the young.

Our job, if it is a job, is to see in each man those great gifts that God has given him. Respect is never out of place—for young or for old.

The shortage of priests and the reforms of Vatican Council II have combined to ease some of the great sources of tension that existed before. The omnipotent pastor who rose to command a "bon ton" parish, and who had as many as four subservient curates, as many as twenty obedient religious sisters, and a completely docile laity, has disappeared.

The question that now must be answered is this. Is the church about to inherit a generation of self-willed, egocentric priests who feel that the world owes them a living?

This I command you: love one another. —John 15:17

He is truly great who is great in charity.
—Thomas à Kempis

Where there is patience and humility, there is neither anger nor worry. —St. Francis of Assisi

It is of great importance that all priests, whether diocesan or regular, should help each other so that they may be fellow helpers of the truth.
—Decree on the Ministry and Life of Priests

A comfortable bachelorhood is no sign of the Kingdom.
—Charles Davis

Collaborative ministry demands the capacity to be rational. —Brother Loughlan Sofield, S.T.

46.

Do not accept an accusation against a presbyter unless it is supported by two or three witnesses.
—1 Timothy 5:19

My brother,

In these days of instant publicity, and innate prejudice on the part of so many against God and his church, how painful it is for the priests of God when our brothers in the priesthood fall into situations of shame and scandal. Their guilt falls upon all of us in some way, and at the very least, their actions reduce our credibility and our effectiveness as instruments of grace.

Individually, of course, we serve God according to our gifts and our vocation. We use our talents to love, serve, and minister to the Christian community.

Therefore, if we are doing our best to shepherd the flock of Christ and to be ambassadors of Christ, we must continue on our course.

As for our brothers who are publicly humiliated by accusation or even indictment, let us pray for them. The bond of the priesthood still holds us. Let us not condemn. There, but for the grace of God, go I.

> Finally, all of you, be of one mind, sympathetic, loving toward one another, compassionate, humble.
> —1 Peter 3:8

> Blessed are the ears which hear God's whisper and listen not to the murmurs of the world.
> —Thomas à Kempis

> Sanctify yourself and you will sanctify society.
> —St. Francis of Assisi

> Priests should be particularly concerned for those [other priests] who are sick, and about those who are afflicted, overworked, lonely, exiled, or persecuted.
> —Decree on the Ministry and Life of Priests

> No quick simple solution exists for the basic challenge facing diocesan priestly life today.
> —George A. Aschenbrenner, S.J.

47.

I charge you before God and Christ Jesus and the elect angels to keep these rules without prejudice, doing nothing out of favoritism. —1 Timothy 5:21

My brother,

The difficulty of being a priest, particularly a parish priest, lies in our call to be at the same time models of holiness, yet part of the flock—*ex animo*—from the heart.

We find ourselves drawn to some and repelled by others. We are driven by our own emotions and reactions to favor certain people and to instinctively repulse others.

This also leads to judgment and prejudice. It is so easy to see guilt in the souls of those we find distasteful and to bear cheerfully with the faults of those we like. Is it not difficult to judge impartially? Yet a further question—Should we judge anyone at all?

Is there politics within the Catholic church? You might as well ask, "Is the pope Catholic?" In fact, how else do we get a pope, if not by election? And any election means candidates. Candidates mean factions, and factions mean politics, as people weigh the merits of the candidates.

Father John Merity, the sage of Jersey City, when speaking of the hierarchical structure of the Archdiocese of Newark, was accustomed to saying, "all the neighbor's children." Meaning, of course, that of the people around the archbishop almost all grew up together with him in the "Oranges" of New Jersey. It was hardly an accident. Nepotism is a time-honored church custom.

For the average priest, there is not much that can be done about the church hierarchy, except to leave it to God. It is his problem.

> . . . because I came down from heaven not to do my own will but the will of the one who sent me.
> —John 6:38

Shepherd the flock by words. Shepherd the flock by the example of your life. —St. Bernard

When a pious and zealous priest has grown completely dead to himself, then he will begin to live the life which Jesus lives on our altars. —Jacques Millet, S.J.

The true minister of Christ is conscious of his own weakness, and labors in humility.
—Decree on the Ministry and Life of Priests

48.

Strive for peace with everyone, and for that holiness without which no one will see the Lord. See to it that no one be deprived of the grace of God, that no bitter root spring up and cause trouble, through which many may become defiled. . . .
—Hebrews 12:14, 15

My brother,

Saint Paul spent his entire Christian life in conflict. Yet, he asks us to strive for peace, while at the same time admonishing us to "see to it" that no man falls away from grace.

People who are being tempted by evil are in a situation of stress. An alcoholic does not want to hear about abstinence. A man in an adulterous relationship does not want to be told about morality.

The sad plight of today's society has come from its abandonment of God. The poison of secularism leads men and women with a worthless value system. The sickness infects all of their hopes and dreams. Their value system is worthless because it begins with the world and ends with the world.

Our peace comes from a pure heart that sees all things as God's and all people as creatures of God.

Peace I leave with you; my peace I give to you. Not as the world gives do I give it to you. Do not let your hearts be troubled or afraid. —John 14:27

. . . even those who let me in don't treat me much better. They usually want everything but what I'm trying to bring. They want to tell me their little cares and worries; they want to pour out their hearts to me. And what a conglomeration comes spilling out! What a disheartening mixture of the comical and the tragic, of small truth and big lies, of little trials that are taken too seriously and big sins that are made light of!
—Karl Rahner, S.J.

To live out of a developed core sense of true self is never easy, especially in our post-modern world, but it is always crucial to responsible, mature living in faith.
—George A. Aschenbrenner, S.J.

49.

I charge [you] before God, who gives life to all things, and before Christ Jesus, who gave testimony under Pontius Pilate for the noble confession, to keep the commandment without stain or reproach until the appearance of our Lord Jesus Christ. —1 Timothy 6:13-14

My brother,
How difficult it is to keep all of God's commandments! Sanctity is the work of a lifetime.

And what makes our progress difficult is that Satan, the master psychologist, attacks us by "blindsiding us."

We are gentle and kind, yet we can be soft and without strength. We can be strong personalities, and we can be without mercy. We can be frugal, and actually be cheap. We can be generous, and yet be wastrels. We can be loving, yet prone to sensuality. We can be without temptation, and yet be puritanical.

If you would find your weakness, my brother, examine your strong points. It is on the flip side of virtue that you will discover your own personal tendency to sin.

There were two pastors in the early 1900s at St. Peter's in Belleville, New Jersey. The first was Father Smith. Everyone loved him. He was gentle, kind, loving, and overweight. He never spoke an unkind word. But when he died, the church and the rectory were in a shambles. He was simply a poor administrator. He was almost ashamed to ask for money.

He was succeeded by Father Fields, who was a thin, "Type A" personality. "A fine thing," he shouted from the pulpit, "The parish priest has to sleep in a rectory where the rain comes through the roof onto his bed." No one liked him, but the buildings were repaired.

They are both buried in the parish cemetery—side by side.

> If we say, "We are without sin," we deceive
> ourselves. . . . —1 John 1:8

> Some priests seem to include in their idea of perfection
> the obligation to live without friends. —Gustav Thils

> Examine your own life daily, as a curious explorer of
> your own integrity. —St. Bernard

50.

. . . the one who judges me is the Lord. —1 Corinthians 4:4

My brother,

Paul had no fear. He was secure in himself. When others disagreed with him, or even took him to task, he stood like a rock.

Why? Because Paul let no deviation from his vocation turn him from his task. He was fully aware of what God wanted. He was unwavering in his one task—to preach Christ, and him crucified.

Do not, brother, let anyone disturb you. Paul did not escape reproach and condemnation. Neither did Jesus.

Therefore, if there are those who are critical of your service of the Lord, just let it bounce off you like raindrops on a rock.

Know that God alone can judge you. Therefore, do not even judge yourself. That is God's work.

"Uncle Pete" was a local character. He had a colorful history. In the Italian neighborhood where he owned a poolroom, Pete was a legend.

When Pete, after some setbacks, decided to come back to church, Father Menagus, the pastor, announced it from the altar. The whole church applauded.

"Uncle Pete" had some advice for a young seminarian. One day in church, he said, "You see those saints, John" (pointing to the statues), "Those saints will never hurt you. But watch out for those living saints. They will get you every time."

Stop judging and you will not be judged. —Luke 6:37

God greatly blesses the labors of those heralds of the gospel who attend first to their own holiness.
—St. Gregory the Great

The totality of the priestly life in the person of the priest has, as its own good, the glorification of the Lord.
—Gustav Thils

Priestly identity implies fidelity to Christ and to the people of God to whom we all are sent.
—Pope John Paul II

A MAN AMONG MEN:
TRYING TO KEEP OUR FOCUS

51.

*Presbyters who preside well deserve double honor, especially
those who toil in preaching and teaching. . . .*

"A worker deserves his pay." —1 Timothy 5:17, 18

My brother,

Questions of our pay, health care benefits, housing, and support are legitimate, my brother.

However, there is no real "merit" system in pay or benefits. The reality is that, in human terms, the laziest, most self-centered priest will receive the same stipend as the zealous, hard-working servant of the Lord.

God's ways are not our ways. We do not labor for filthy lucre. We who serve in the wealthy world are bound to serve with a modest lifestyle. Otherwise, we are a scandal and a bad example to the faithful.

If we serve in a poor area, or in the Third World, we must be content with whatever physical rewards we receive. To be much more content and better off than the flock would cause them to question our lifestyle and our motives.

The young priest of today should be conscious of the debt that he owes to those good priests and bishops of the post-Vatican Council II era, who struggled to improve the lot of the average priest.

How many priests today would be happy with a salary of $75 a month, one day off a week (when they had to be home by midnight), no car allowance, where being on duty meant answering the phone, writing Mass cards and certificates, answering the door, and above all being available twenty-four hours a day in the house? Oh, yes, they got three weeks of vacation, once a year. The benefits that priests enjoy today were not easily won.

> So do not worry and say, "What are we to eat?" or "What are we to drink?" or "What are we to wear?" All these things the pagans seek. —Matthew 6:31–32

> All the aspects of the priestly ministry bear the distinctive mark of sacrifice. —Jean Galot, S.J.

> Poverty is the door to freedom because, finding nothing in ourselves that is a source of hope, we know that there is nothing in ourselves worth defending. We go out of ourselves, therefore, to rest in Him, in whom alone is our hope. —Thomas Merton

> A priest should live on the same level as his people. —Raymond A. Tartre, S.S.S.

52.

"Everything is lawful," but not everything is beneficial.
"Everything is lawful," but not everything builds up. No one
should seek his own advantage, but that of his neighbor.
—1 Corinthians 10:23, 24

My brother,

We live in full view of the world. No priest is without constant surveillance by the people around him.

A scandal caused by a priest is a stumbling block to someone's belief in the church and in its Christ.

Priests must be cautious of their deportment, their language, their opinions. The most difficult concept to embrace is this: a priest has no strictly private or personal life. He is a representative of the church—and more, of Jesus himself. Even if a priest is asleep in his rectory, even if he is on vacation, even if he is out of sight of all people, he is still a public figure. A priest is essentially a *mediator Dei*, one who stands between God and the world.

And so, my friend, when you look in the mirror, you are seeing the face of God's man on earth. Tough but true.

Just so, your light must shine before others, that they
may see your good deeds and glorify your heavenly
Father. —Matthew 5:16

A priest, when he goes among men, should be a ray of
sunshine which is never fully detached from its source.
—Jacques Millet, S.J.

Priests have an obligation of showing people that
sanctification can be the heritage of all those who
respond to grace. —Gustav Thils

The pastor must be pure in thought, exemplary in his
actions, discreet in his silence, and useful in his words.
He should be close to all in compassion, and, above all,
be dedicated to contemplation. He should be the
humble ally of all who do good.
—The Priest and the Third Christian Millennium

It's unavoidable: Your official business and my private
life cannot be separated. —Karl Rahner, S.J.

53.

*We cause no one to stumble in anything, in order that no
fault may be found with our ministry. . . .*
—2 Corinthians 6:3

My brother,
    In government, they call it diplomacy. In business, they call
it tact. In society, they call it courtesy.
    Years ago, the long intense seminary formation was more
than just spiritual and intellectual formation. The church literally took young people, rich and poor, and formed them cul-
turally and attitudinally.
    Polite manners were required to be ordained, as were clean-
liness, hygiene, and proper decorum. Rough and uncouth

young people became priests—men of learning, men of the best in personal mannerisms.

Today, the seminary is apt to focus only on education and some spiritual formation. The result is a very mixed group of clergy.

The priest should be a true Renaissance man, a man at home in any setting—among any group of people—a man among men.

In today's society, where image and appearance mean so much, it hardly does the church a great deal of good when the priest, the representative of the organization, is a boor, a loud-mouth, disheveled in his attire, malodorous in body, of bad breath, or afflicted with indecorous bodily actions. John Merity, in the days of many priests in one rectory, would say to one of the brothers at meal time humorously, "Why don't you eat on the back porch?" And then he would follow with this line, "And his mother is such a nice person."

> But the wise shall shine brightly
>   like the splendor of the firmament,
> And those who lead the many to justice
>   shall be like the stars forever. —Daniel 12:3

The priest cannot allow the center of his being to gravitate excessively to the human side so as to obscure his priesthood. Neither must he move to the other side to become so dehumanized as to be reduced to a caricature. After all, his nature will never allow him to be an angel. So above all, he must achieve a balance.
—Frederico Suarez

The priest must be graced by no less knowledge and culture than is usual among well-bred and well-educated of his day. That is to say, he must be healthily modern. —Pope Pius XI

54.

Remember your leaders who spoke the word of God to you.
Consider the outcome of their way of life and imitate their
faith. Jesus Christ is the same yesterday, today, and forever.
Do not be carried away by all kinds of strange teaching. It is
good to have our hearts strengthened by grace and not by
foods, which do not benefit those who live by them.
—Hebrews 13:7–9

My brother,

The seminary is a place of formation. It reflects the faith of
the church. That faith is formed and reinforced in the young
men as they work their way to the goal of the priesthood.

The dogma of the church is strong food—the meat and pota-
toes of spiritual nourishment. Those teachings of our church
are not merely empty statements full of wind and smoke. Our
very salvation rests on their reality.

Why follow foolishness? What can watered-down teachings
do for us? They have no spiritual power to move us to greater
union with God. They are without stability.

Remember the seminary! Remember your holy professors!
What they were to you then, you are now to others. Feed your
flock the truth!

> If you remain in my word, you will truly be my
> disciples. . . . —John 8:31

> The priest cannot consistently and correctly preach the
> faith unless he himself is deeply grounded in it.
> —Aloysius Biskupek, S.V.D.

> Dogma is the only proper foundation for devotion.
> Without it, we are mere sentimentalists.
> —Eugene Boylan, O.C.R.

> A sacred minister's knowledge ought to be sacred, in
> the sense that it is derived from a sacred source and
> directed to a sacred purpose.
> —Decree on the Ministry and Life of Priests

The Gospel preached by the church is not just a
message, but a divine and life-giving experience for
those who believe, hear, receive and obey the message.
—The Priest in the Third Christian Millennium

55.

*. . . so that we may no longer be infants, tossed by waves and
swept along by every wind of teaching arising from human
trickery, from their cunning in the interests of deceitful
scheming.* —Ephesians 4:14

My brother,

Paul certainly knew human nature. Look around you! See all
of the varieties of Christianity. Think of all of the twists and
turns of theological innovation that have occurred—especially
after Vatican Council II. How many movements have been
born, flourished, and then disappeared? Whether teachings are
liberal or conservative, whether teachings are new age or fos-
silized legends, only the truth has staying power.

So many young, zealous, and holy priests have become
intoxicated with novelties and, following their own lights,
have ended up in strange places. How many have left their
true calling and now languish in a drab secular world? Their
path led away from their early ideals to a much different
world.

We must always be truthful. Whatever is, is. All things must
be tested. A man may move on. But it should always be
according to his own assessment—not according to some
opinion created by someone else and resting on an unreality
that is merely a myth or a dream.

> Blessed are you, O LORD;
> teach me your laws.
> With my lips I recite
> All the edicts you have spoken. —Psalms 119:12–13

Of what benefit to souls can be the discourses of preachers who do not prepare themselves for their work by study and prayer. —Jacques Millet, S.J.

The gospel contains as many mysteries as words and each mystery of faith constitutes a lifetime's work. —St. Jerome

No mature person expects a permanent commitment to be easy. —George A. Aschenbrenner, S.J.

The love of truth means perpetual childhood, fresh and joyful. —Pope John XXIII

56.

When I was a child, I used to talk as a child, think as a child, reason as a child; when I became a man, I put aside childish things. —1 Corinthians 13:11

My brother,

Let us never think that we are so mature that our younger character has left us completely. We are what we are. We have our own temperaments, our own likes and dislikes, our own genetic makeups, and our own experiences.

The boy that you once were still lies just under your skin. We may have layers and layers of training, discipline, and even penitential resignation added to and covering the personality you thought you had lost—the young man of long ago.

So, if that old personality breaks forth now and then and you perhaps act like the character you thought you had lost—don't be surprised. We may have put childish ways aside, but we can't put our own intrinsic nature aside.

We can channel our lives. We can mold and shape our mannerisms. But we must always be aware that there is that inner core within us that defies all efforts to make it disappear. It is the self and, to tell the truth, that's not bad.

For the Father himself loves you, because you have loved Me. . . . —John 16:27

Just as Christ on the cross loved me, and delivered himself up for me, so here too he loves me and comes to me in the Blessed Sacrament. When He finds himself united to me in communion, He is by no means surprised to learn that I am a sinner. He knew that before and loved me as I am. —Thomas Merton

You ask only for our wills that our souls should be prepared as wax to receive your seal. —Gerard Straub

It is not the results of our own speculation, but the golden harvest of what we have lived through and suffered through, that has power to enrich the heart and nourish the spirit. —Karl Rahner, S.J.

57.

Avoid profane, idle talk, for such people will become more and more godless, and their teaching will spread like gangrene.
—2 Timothy 2:16, 17

My brother,

We in religious life are more apt than others to engage in gossip. The reason is simple. We deal with people. We are engaged in all the facets of ordinary everyday life.

Therefore, while we serve the Lord and strive for holiness, we cannot escape the flock. Nor should we.

But since people, in a sense, are our business, we can become very judgmental in our attitudes. Subconsciously, we rate people. We know the saint and the sinner. We know the worker from the talker. We soon can evaluate the persons who are real and distinguish them from the ones who are ambitious and pretentious.

Also, we love to talk about our confreres in the church. We like to know who is where, who is ill, who is doing well, who has problems.

In other words, one of the great penances we can and should practice is tending to our own business. It does not help others to spread the news about their personal lives.

I once went on a retreat. Quite by accident, I found myself among a group of very well-known clergy. They were, in fact, celebrities of radio and television. Some were authors. All were considered holy men and conservative theologians.

I sat quietly at meals for a week as I listened to these gentlemen deride, laugh at, scorn, and make jokes at the expense of their opposites—well-known liberals. They were certainly righteous and pure. But they knew nothing of charity.

> . . . and [he] did not need anyone to testify about human nature. He himself understood it well.
> —John 2:25

> The only tragedy is that we are all not saints.
> —Charles Peguy

> One of the first things you must learn if you want to be a contemplative, is how to mind your own business.
> —Thomas Merton

58.

Avoid foolish arguments, genealogies, rivalries, and quarrels about the law, for they are useless and futile. —Titus 3:9

My brother,

Have you ever looked back and considered how many and what type of arguments have occurred in your life? If you analyze them at a later time, you will often discover that they were mostly over trivial things, and were, in the long run, nonproductive and pointless. Some, in fact, may have been embarrassing. In short, Paul may have been perfectly correct. They were stupid.

That is not to say that we must not have opinions or even feel strongly about concepts, ideas, events, or even personalities. The difficulty lies in permitting our passions to override reason.

The mark of a mature man is his ability to reason, to discern, and to analyze. In short, the ideal of the priest is that wise sage who judges all things with equanimity, and who tempers all judgments with charity.

Let us pray each day for wisdom. It is the manifestation of holiness.

Have you ever thought about the fact that Jesus was opposed by two primary factions? One was the Pharisees, the ultra-conservative Jews who had built a "fence around the law," and by doing so had imprisoned the Jewish people in a religious straightjacket. The other group was the Sadducees, the (priestly) crowd who obeyed only what they had to. They were theologically liberal.

The only time they ever combined forces was to attack Jesus. He was too conservative for the liberals, and too liberal for the conservatives. So you go and be likewise.

For she [Wisdom] is the refulgence of eternal light,
the spotless mirror of the power of God,
the image of his goodness. —Wisdom 7:26

The priest should be courteous, well mannered, friendly, and polite to everyone. —Frederico Suarez

Worldly speech in a priest may achieve popularity; it will never achieve respect. —Eugene Boylan, O.C.R.

Wiseacres may show disrespect, if not scorn, for the simple man. But those wiseacres are of no account . . . no notice should be taken of them at all.
—Pope John XXIII

59.

So turn from youthful desires and pursue righteousness,
faith, love, and peace, along with those who call on the Lord
with purity of heart. Avoid foolish and ignorant debates, for
you know that they breed quarrels. —2 Timothy 2:22, 23

My brother,

Notice how Saint Paul connects senseless, useless, ignorant disputations with youth and passion.

The pure heart sees all things clearly. A youthful heart that is filled with love and peace will often understand things more clearly than an older heart that has been corroded by sins, prejudices, and hatred.

Jesus said, "Let the children come to me, and do not prevent them; for the kingdom of heaven belongs to such as these" (Mt 19:14). He was not speaking of age—or of childishness. He was referring to the unspoiled soul who has avoided temptations that distort the vision of the soul and produce a clouded vision of reality.

My brother, your daily examination of conscience, your frequent confessions, are the balm for your soul and the corrective of your innate tendencies. The grace of God will help to quiet your passions—and to avoid confrontations.

> How I love your teaching, Lord!
> I study it all day long.
> —Psalms 119:97

The preparation of the man is far more important than the preparation of the sermon. —Eugene Boylan, O.C.R.

Man can give to God nothing greater than to submit his will to God because of God. —St. Thomas Aquinas

> All priestly existence undergoes an inexorable decline,
> if the priest, through negligence or whatever other
> reason, neglects frequent recourse, inspired by faith and
> devotion to the Sacrament of Penance. If a priest no
> longer goes to confession or makes a bad confession,
> this will affect his priestly ministry and be noticed by
> the community of which he is pastor.
> —The Priest and the Third Christian Millennium

60.

So whether you eat or drink, or whatever you do, do
everything for the glory of God. Avoid giving offense,
whether to Jews or Greeks or the church of God. . . .
—1 Corinthians 10:31, 32

My brother,

It may seem strange that Paul would single out food and drink as means to honor God.

The answer is, of course, that Paul was showing that all of our activities—even ordinary, necessary ones such as eating and drinking—can be occasions of giving glory to God. It is very similar to the act of consecration to the Sacred Heart— "Oh Jesus, I offer you my prayers, works, joys, and sufferings of this day."

Yet, that is why a total consecration of our lives is important. So often it is the "little things" that either glorify or offend God. Hindu and Buddhist spirituality has the characteristic of focusing life and attention on all of the tiny details of life—and then using them to achieve union with God. Should we not in some way imitate their path of perfection?

Unless you are a monk or a hermit, being present to the moment is never easy for a busy priest. Half of the time, we live in the future, trying to plan, to discern, to arrange our lives. The other half of the time, we live in the past, reliving the things that happened. "Now" is difficult. But it is all the nows put together that constitute our lives.

Come to me, all you who labor and are burdened, and I will give you rest. —Matthew 11:28

Lifting up the mind to God is in most cases not as easy as it might seem. —Aloysius Biskupek, S.V.D.

Clerics should lead a holier outer and inner life than the laity and provide better example in virtue and good works. —Roman Pontifical

Priests are so deeply occupied in dealing with the trees that they have no time to locate a vantage point from which to see the extent and shape of the forest that surrounds them. —Most Reverend Thomas J. Curry

61.

Say these things. Exhort and correct with all authority. Let no one look down on you. —Titus 2:15

My brother,

Herein lies a challenge and a cross for you.

As a priest of God, you have no choice but to speak God's words and to reinforce God's commands.

Often, you will find yourself struggling against the current stream of modern day morality. The world will not like you. The world did not accept the prophets of God in any age. Nor did they accept Jesus.

Our struggle is against the world, the flesh, and the devil. Our ways are not the world's ways. We stand for an invisible God, and a spiritual standard of conduct that stands on natural law and a theological morality that requires a higher standard than that of the secular world.

There will always be resistance. But you, my friend, must stand in the breach. You are the brass wall to defend God's law.

It is the same with church laws. It will always be most difficult for a pastor who does his best to follow the rules and norms of the universal and local church, especially when there are other parishes nearby where those very same rules and norms are simply ignored. Let's face it. If you do the right thing, you will often have to pay a price. It often means being disliked.

> If you belonged to the world, the world would love its own; but because you do not belong to the world, and I have chosen you out of the world, the world hates you.
> —John 15:19

The priestly life is a struggle waged with perseverance against the evil spirit. —Gustav Thils

Holy denotes the man who is set aside from the profane so as to belong totally to God, and be consecrated to Him. —E. Schlussler Fiorenza

Sacerdotem etenim praesse (Romans Pont.). It is fitting for the priest to be a leader. It is necessary, therefore, for the priest to have charge, to direct, to watch, to defend, and to encourage. "Praesse" is an essential obligation. —Aloysius Biskupek, S.V.D.

62.

Indeed, religion with contentment is a great gain. For we brought nothing into the world, just as we shall not be able to take anything out of it. If we have food and clothing, we shall be content with that. Those who want to be rich are falling into temptation and into a trap and into many foolish and harmful desires, which plunge them into ruin and destruction. For the love of money is the root of all evils, and some people in their desire for it have strayed from the faith and have pierced themselves with many pains.

But you, man of God, avoid all this. Instead, pursue righteousness, devotion, faith, love, patience, and gentleness. Compete well for the faith. —1 Timothy 6:6–12

My brother,

Many, many priests over the years have fallen into the trap of envy and greed. Still others have sought the companionship of the rich and the famous.

How easy and delightful it can be to spend time with the well-bred and the wealthy, the witty, and the powerful. But what can they bring into our lives? Are not the rich and distinguished themselves merely human? Many live empty lives following ephemeral fame and fortune, their lives devoid of true spirituality.

Seek first the kingdom of God. Take pleasure in the company of the wise and righteous. Especially, if you are able, discover the spiritual friend who shares your true values. You are not of this world.

There are now, always have been, and always will be, within the ranks of the clergy, the "climbers."

If there is a dinner, or a cocktail party, or a social event, where important people are present, they are there. If the bishop, or bishops, are present at a function, they are there. Little do they realize that truly important people recognize what they are doing. Instead of being admired, the world sees them as sad figures—"wannabes" is the word that describes them.

> . . . I, the Lord, your God, who have set you apart from the other nations. —Leviticus 20:24

> The Son of God loves silence, solitude, and recollection, but you are ever in the midst of excitement, toil, and tumult. —Jacques Millet, S.J.

> Every priest should be a man of the heart, a man with a big heart, but his mind should govern his actions. —Frederico Suarez

63.

I know indeed how to live in humble circumstances; I know also how to live with abundance. In every circumstance and in all things I have learned the secret of being well fed and of going hungry, of living in abundance and of being in need. I have the strength for everything through him who empowers me. —Philippians 4:12–13

My brother,

What a great gift it is to be indifferent to the world around you. If you seek comfort and consolation from others, you will more often than not find that those very "others" have their own troubles. They will have very little to give you.

So, courage and fortitude are the rare commodities that the spiritual athlete needs to run the course.

In a more practical vein, are you content with the small pleasures in a priest's life? Can you live the simple life, eating ordinary food, enjoying good books and music, being content with good times spent with dear friends? It is good for a priest to have a hobby or a recreation that he truly enjoys, and especially one that refreshes his soul.

A comedian, Joe E. Lewis, once said, "I've been rich and I've been poor. And believe me, rich is better." And in absolute terms, he was correct.

However, a priest must not live a life of luxury. It is a scandal that injures the very image of the priest.

Take nothing for the journey, neither walking stick, nor sack, nor food, nor money, and let no one take a second tunic. Whatever house you enter, stay there and leave from there. —Luke 9:3, 4

Contact with the world and detachment from the world are not compatible. To be pitied is the priest who must seek contact with the world because he cannot find contentment in the friendship of the Lord.
—Aloysius Biskupek, S.V.D.

Perfection is found principally in the love of God and secondarily in the love of neighbor.
—Reginald Garrigou-Logrange

To live, supported by others, like landed gentry, would destroy any witness to a simple lifestyle to God's love for us all. —George A. Aschenbrenner, S.J.

THE CHRISTIAN IDEAL: THE MAN WHO TRIES EVEN WHEN HE FAILS

64.

. . . so that one who belongs to God may be competent, equipped for every good work. —2 Timothy 3:17

My brother,

Our education does not, and cannot, end at ordination. The priest of today must be intelligent, well read, and well versed in spirituality and theology.

That means that from the day of ordination until the day he is called to God, a priest is always a student—a disciple of Christ.

How sad it is when the priest of God stands in the pulpit and merely mouths a trite and hackneyed ideology with no research, no variety, and no true message.

Someone will suffer when we preach. Either we suffer as we work to prepare our sermon, or the people will suffer as they listen to us.

The electronic media is not enough. A well-read priest is essential if he is to meet today's educated lay person and bring Christ into his life.

> Since you have rejected knowledge,
> I will reject you from my priesthood. . . . —Hosea 4:6

Some study simply to acquire knowledge. This is curiosity. Some study to gain a reputation. This is vanity. Some study to make of their knowledge a commercial commodity. This is lust for money. Others use knowledge to rise to places of eminence. This is

ambition. Some, however, study for self instruction.
This is prudence. And some there are who study that
they may be able to instruct others, and this is charity.
—St. Bernard

The Catholic priest is set up as a leader in Israel.
—St. Gregory the Great

Holiness does not suffice to the modern priest; he must
be fully equipped intellectually in order to meet on an
equal footing the progressively higher standards of
college education of today's men and women.
—Raymond A. Tartre, S.S.S.

The Gospel preached by the church is not just a
message, but a divine and life-giving experience for
those who believe, hear, receive, and obey the message.
—The Priest and the Third Christian Millennium

65.

*We have not received the spirit of the world but the Spirit
that is from God, so that we may understand the things freely
given us by God.* —1 Corinthians 2:12

My brother,
   How many gifts there are among us. There are priests who
are by nature wise and intelligent. Others are instinctively kind
and generous. There are those who are witty and good-
humored. Others are serious and compassionate. Some make a
fine appearance. Others make people feel comfortable.
   The reality is that most priests have a combination of innate
talents and abilities.
   The problem is that often priests have a tendency to see only
their faults and their weaknesses. My friend, if God has called
you to his service, he has also fitted you for the role you are to
play in his plan of salvation.
   Who you are is more important than what you do. The Holy
Spirit, abiding within you, will, if you permit him, mold your

spirit and guide your life. You are the instrument of God in the world.

When I was a boy, we had a fife, drum, and bugle corps. One boy wanted desperately to belong. He tried the fife. He tried the bugle. It was impossible for him. He tried the drums. He was too uncoordinated.

Then, one of the instructors tried him on the bass drum. That kid was like an automated machine. He gave exactly 120 beats a minute. He was perfect.

. . . Do you love me? . . . Feed my sheep. —John 21:17

The priest, a consecrated man, has a special quality, the quality of something holy for his sacramental consecration endows him with a special character.
—Frederico Suarez

The priesthood is the embodiment of God's love for men. —Aloysius Biskupek, S.V.D.

One can have a profound sense of dissatisfaction with one's own limitations and the disparity between one's own ideals and achievement, and nevertheless be profoundly fulfilled in striving for a goal.
—Most Reverend Thomas J. Curry

66.

Brothers, stop being childish in your thinking. In respect to evil be like infants, but in your thinking be mature.
—1 Corinthians 14:20

My brother,

Jesus said, "Let the children come to me, and do not prevent them; for the kingdom of heaven belongs to such as these" (Mt 19:14).

However, childishness is different from being childlike. Children can be petulant, selfish, stubborn, demanding, and in general, they can be a nuisance to others. Their world is wrapped up in their own needs and desires.

How sad it is when priests act like petulant children. How many fall away from the spiritual ideals of the seminary to become almost completely wrapped up in their own well-being.

Brothers, we must be big men. I do not mean in size. We must be larger in spirit. We cannot permit small incidents, or people who are diminutive in soul, to affect us. A grown-up priest is a blessing to the community. He does not have his own interest at heart. He is God's man among the people.

However, being a "big" person does not enable a priest to escape from the nonsense of ordinary life. In other words, grown-up people often act like children.

One parish erupted in a verbal war in the 1960s over the clothing that girls could wear for confirmation. When the nun said "no" to pantsuits, there was a meeting of parents that almost ended in a riot.

The pastor had to sit through it all. Finally, the compromise was a "confirmation gown" that, like charity, "covered all sins." There are times when a priest needs the wisdom of Solomon and the patience of Job.

Your priests will be clothed with justice;
    your faithful will shout for joy.
—Psalms 132:9

Priests are concerned with affirming mysterious
realities of which they say they are eyewitnesses for
they walk with their eyes open to the deific light.
—St. Benedict

As a shepherd, the priest is called to make Christ
present in the community. —Jean Galot, S.J.

67.

. . . but everything must be done properly and in order.
—1 Corinthians 14:40

My brother,
 What a cross the administrative work of today's ministry can be.
 We do not just "give" sacraments. We are responsible for the preparation and education of the faithful. There is often paperwork and details of preparation to be worked out. There are rehearsals and arrangements of all types to make certain that all things are done properly.
 In truth, Jesus and the apostles never had to deal with the minutiae—and often the nonsense—that priests do in today's world.
 Yet, there is no way to avoid the fact that the church is an institution. It has rules, guidelines, and like any business, records to keep. Perhaps some, in monasteries and religious orders, can escape the drudgery of everyday corporate work. But for most of us, there it sits. It is part of our job description. It can only be spiritual gold if we do it properly.
 Before Vatican Council II, there was very little communication between the diocese and the parish. In fact, there was a rule that three days were needed to get certain dispensations. If it took more time, the priest, in certain circumstances, could go ahead.
 Since Vatican Council II, there are a multitude of diocesan agencies. Each must prove its worth by the amount of paper it creates. By a letter, then a fax, now by Internet (e-mail), the messages, like the ocean tide, pour in from headquarters. The pastor's manual alone is immense and continues to grow. Some day, we may all drown in paper. Until then, do the best that you can and use the "circular file" with discretion.

 . . . so be shrewd as serpents and simple as doves.
 —Matthew 10:16

The diocesan priest is increasingly absorbed in material tasks: attendance at funerals, burials, and marriages; bookkeeping; material responsibility for activities which lead him to lose sight of the essentially supernatural goal of his apostolate.
—The Diocesan Clergy Face to Face With Its Evangelizing Mission (French, 1945)

The apostolate, regardless of the form in which it presents itself, constitutes at all times for the apostle a means of sanctification. —Dom Chautard

Unlike those rulers and teachers of old, Your modern stewards have imposed heavy burdens not only on others, but on themselves too. —Karl Rahner, S.J.

68.

And whatever you do, in word or in deed, do everything in the name of the Lord Jesus, giving thanks to God the Father through him. —Colossians 3:17

My brother,

Almost every priest of earlier generations began his day with the morning offering to the Sacred Heart. The prayer gave focus to each and every action of our day.

More importantly, our daily offering of the holy liturgy brings our priesthood to its essential character—the priestly role of sacrifice.

Monsignor Bill Hogan, a devout priest and a good theologian, told his seminary students that, when they were ordained, they might find themselves jumping out of bed, running into the sacristy and on to the altar to say Mass. "If you do so," he said, "no one will say anything, but you will not be giving God nor the Mass its due."

Before Vatican Council II, every priest said certain prayers while he donned the sacred vestments. These prayers had the effect of fixing the mind on the holiness and serious nature of what we were about. After Mass also, almost every priest knelt at a prie-dieu to offer thanksgiving. Sadly these things are gone now.

Should we not celebrate each Mass as if it were our last? What care and love is needed to properly unite our hearts to the Lord Jesus as we "do this in commemoration of him."

> . . . Do this in memory of me. —Luke 22:19

> The Liturgy is the summit toward which the activity of the Church is directed. Pastors themselves [must] become thoroughly penetrated with the spirit and power of the Liturgy and become masters of it.
> —Sacerdatalis Coelibatus

> As teachers and rulers, priests act only in the name of Christ, while in the celebration of the Mass, they act in the person of Christ. —Cardinal Suhard

> What distinguishes the ministry of the priest . . . is that it is exercised . . . to reach the supreme moment when, standing at the altar of God, the priest offers the people with Christ and enables them to offer themselves as an agreeable sacrifice to the glory and worship of the Father. —Raymond A. Tartre, S.S.S.

69.

And over all these put on love, that is, the bond of perfection.
—Colossians 3:14

My brother,

Here we are at the summary of the way of holiness. The final note is *caritas*—love. The final word is love. The final decision we make is to love.

You are a priest. Your life is love. It is not romance, or dreamy imagination. Your love is far more. Your love is Christ, the one who said, "No one has greater love than this, to lay down one's life for one's friends" (Jn 15:13).

You, priest of God, if you persevere, will have laid down your life for the greatest of friends—the Lord Jesus Christ. You are his. He is yours. Your eternity will be filled with love—the everlasting radiance of God.

In the old ritual, in assisting at mixed marriages, the priest had an exhortation for the couple that read in part,

> And so not knowing what is before you, you take each other for better or for worse, for richer or for poorer, in sickness and in health, until death.
>
> Truly, then, these words are most serious . . . and, because these words involve such solemn obligations, it is most fitting then that you rest the security of your wedded life upon the great principle of self-sacrifice. . . . Sacrifice is usually difficult and irksome. Only love can make it easy; and perfect love can make it a joy. We are willing to give in proportion as we love, And when love is perfect, the sacrifice is complete.

Should not these words apply to us—the priests of God?

> God is love, and whoever remains in love remains in God. . . . —1 John 4:16

> Among those who distinguish themselves, men love most those who distinguish themselves by love.
> —Aristotle

> To rejoice to thee, over thee, and for thee, and nothing else is the everlasting blessed life. —St. Augustine

> On the tree of the cross, the Heart of Jesus beheld your heart and loved it. —St. Francis de Sales

70.

Therefore, whoever thinks he is standing secure should take care not to fall. No trial has come to you but what is human. God is faithful and will not let you be tried beyond your strength; but with the trial he will also provide a way out, so that you may be able to bear it. —1 Corinthians 10:12, 13

My brother,

"God will not let you be tempted beyond your strength." What an ironic statement for those of us who try and try, and yet fall and fall again.

Theoretically, yes, God will not let us be tempted above our strength. But in reality, our own weakness of disposition almost guarantees that we are in fact going to fail on many counts and, in many areas of holiness, often our own strength can become our weakness.

And there is also another reality. Any man who thinks he is perfect is fooling himself. The difference between the sinner and the saint is often not a great one. Great saints and great sinners are people of passion and desire. The very ardor of their spirit can lead them across the divide in either direction.

We, poor mediocre souls that we are, are left somewhere in the middle. We are not so evil as to be condemned. But we are not so holy as to be admirable.

So, my brother, while God says that he will not tempt us beyond our strength, take comfort in the fact that most of us are not that strong to begin with. A little breath of adversity— and we are blown over. But God loves us anyway.

The devil is an "equal opportunity" tempter. He has no regard for age, occupation, or status. The old adage among priests, that the temptations of the flesh "die three days after you do," may not be too much of an exaggeration after all.

. . . but he who listens will finally have his say.
—Proverbs 21:28

Of my priests, my elect, and chosen ones, I ask once more all their love, and that they should never, never doubt mine. —Jesus to St. Josefa Menendez

For all those who call upon it, the sacramental grace of ordination will keep intact the immaculate splendor and divine radiance of the gift which is the priesthood. —Gustav Thils

71.

We know that all things work for good for those who love God, who are called according to his purpose. —Romans 8:28

My brother,

Saint Paul never gave us more helpful words than these. For those who love God, all things work together unto good.

It may seem unreal or even a lie to speak in this way when things go bad. Horrible, awful things can occur to human beings along the road of life.

But we must remember that we cannot judge things now as we see them. For God's ways are not our ways; God has his own agenda.

One thing we must cling to. One thing we must believe. God loves us. He desires only our good—our eternal salvation first—and then our spiritual growth here.

We must learn Job's lesson. "The Lord gave and the Lord has taken away; blessed be the name of the Lord!" (Jb 1:21). The present sorrows are as nothing compared to the good that God has laid up for us in the kingdom of heaven.

And truthfully, if we are faithful, we shall have all good here and heaven too.

In a variation of an old song, "It's easy to smile when life's worthwhile and life goes by like a song. But the man worthwhile is the man who can smile when all things have gone dead wrong."

It's all a matter of perspective, of "mind over matter." For the Christian, for the priest, perspective is everything. When and if we arrive at the heavenly homeland, we can ask the martyrs all about it.

> Your Father knows what you need before you ask him.
> —Matthew 6:8

> Christ is our wisest and best friend.
> —St. Thomas Aquinas

> There is only one problem on which all my existence, my peace, and my happiness depends—to discover myself in discovering God. If I find Him, I will find myself. If I find my true self, I will find Him.
> —Thomas Merton

> Each moment of our lives is like a grain of sand lying just alongside the ocean of mystery. —Karl Rahner, S.J.

72.

So with yourselves: since you strive eagerly for spirits, seek to have an abundance of them for building up the church.
—1 Corinthians 14:12

My brother,

One of the most difficult of all virtues is that of acceptance. Almost every priest, at one time or another, has felt the desire to do some special work for God. Many priests would say that they are "moved by the Spirit."

It could be a desire to teach in a school. It could be a wish to become an itinerant preacher in the diocese—or even the country. It could be an inner call to evangelize, or to create a special ministry for youth or the aged. It might be a call to drop all else and to pursue personal holiness.

But reality intervenes. The people of God need us. They need their priests for the express purpose of ministry—Mass, sacraments, spiritual care of the faithful. We do not have the luxury of becoming "specialists." In the spiritual world, most of us are general practitioners. Only a few can realize the goal of a very unique and individualized ministry.

Even those within specific ministries—e.g., theology, prison, campus, or hospital ministry, chancery or tribunal work—at times can find their lives confining and unfulfilling.

But God's work must go on, my brother. We cannot do it "our way." It must be "his" way, if we are to be effective ministers for the Lord.

> I glorified you on earth by accomplishing the work that you gave me to do. —John 17:4

> Priests are "spiritual physicians experienced in the art of healing men by the power from on high" and they must be such throughout their entire lives.
> —Gustav Thils (on the Order of Exorcist)

> The new sacred is intended, not to rescue the profane from all divine ascendancy, but to effect the most fundamental sacralization of it. Sacralization is meant to extend to the whole fabric of man, and to the whole world. —Jean Galot, S.J.

> When our security is too rooted in a job, or a place, or even a certain reputation, there results a stubborn rigidity, just as availability can equally be undermined by a disordered need for change and variety—as when we are so superficially committed that we really don't care whether we are changed or where we are assigned.
> —George A. Aschenbrenner, S.J.

> St. Teresa of Avila had an ecstasy while frying fish.
> —Thomas Vernon Moore, M.D., Carthusian

73.

For God is the one who, for his good purpose, works in you both to desire and to work. —Philippians 2:13

My brother,

Beware of false contentment. Whether we are just ordained or a fifty-year veteran of the priesthood, there should be some restlessness within us—a desire to do a little more for God.

A complete contentment that is merely a mask for self-indulgence and torpid laziness is a great danger. A priest is always a priest.

Even were we in a situation of illness or in a nursing home, a priest can evangelize simply by example. He can do good works by offering his pain each day to God.

The holy priest is a gift from God to the world. His inner peace and his serene countenance is not a simple state of being. It is the fruit of a life united to God.

There is always an inner energy in the soul of the just man. It is a movement for the transcendent—an instinct for the creator—a reaching for God. Those who love God are filled with life.

> . . . therefore God, your God, has anointed you
> with the oil of gladness above your fellow kings.
> —Psalms 45:8

> Zeal is a burning flame, lighted at the hearth of heaven,
> which melts the heart of the apostolic man.
> —William of Paris

> If all priests were saints, they would spread through all
> the earth divine fire. —Jacques Millet, S.J.

> Simplicity is a value and a virtue that radiates from the
> heart of God and glows on the face of Jesus the High
> Priest. —George A. Aschenbrenner, S.J.

> Every priest is another Christ in a special, very real
> way. Each priest is related to every other priest in
> Christ. —Raymond A. Tartre, S.S.S.

DRIVEN BY LOVE: OUR PRIMARY MOTIVATION

74.

. . . the love of Christ impels us. . . . —2 Corinthians 5:14

My brother,

The influence of the Holy Spirit of God is everywhere. It is manifest primarily within the soul by the creation of a fire—the fire of love.

Priests have a difficulty expressing this love. The male nature does not lend itself to such emotions that are often so easily a part of the female.

The love of Christ is powerful. It can make men act with a courage far beyond their natural strength. For example, it is part of a warrior's code to love a comrade in arms. To fight, and even to die, for a fellow soldier is more than an ideal. It is part of common valor in a disciplined army.

How much more should we be driven by the love of Christ to give and to spend ourselves in his church! Our goal is the sanctification of the world. Our enemies are the world, the flesh, and the devil. It is easier to hide and do nothing.

Yet, the love of Christ drives us to serve him and to give ourselves day by day to God's people. It is our call. It is Christ that impels us.

> *. . . for whoever is begotten by God conquers the world. And the victory that conquers the world is our faith.* —1 John 5:4

> The brotherhood of priests comes together supernaturally in Christ who is the brother of all. —Jean Galot, S.J.

The unity of the clergy is basically rooted in the common spirit of pastoral charity. —Gustav Thils

All priests share with the bishops the one identical priesthood and ministry of Christ.
—Decree on the Ministry and Life of Priests

Heralds of the Gospel are needed who are expert in humanity, profoundly knowing the heart of contemporary man, who share his joys and hopes, his fears and sorrows, and, at the same time, who are contemplatives in love with God.
—The Priest and the Third Christian Millennium

75.

I will most gladly spend and be utterly spent for your sakes. If I love you more, am I to be loved less?
—2 Corinthians 12:15

My brother,

Paul speaks in terms of the inner spirit that drives him.

The love that first moved him never diminished. Like the Lord, Paul was often an unrequited lover. He traveled incessantly. He taught. He argued. He cajoled. Many times he was greeted with coldness and indifference. Many times he met open hostility. The physical abuse he suffered, by his own account, was enormous.

Yet, driven by God's love, he could not take "no" for an answer.

Yes, in a sense, he loved too much. He loved to the point of being at times unreasonable.

Do we not give up too easily? How many, many priests have spent their lives in hostile surroundings? How many holy men have given all their energy to people—only to be ignored, or even despised?

Can we love too much? Never, my brothers. Never! If you doubt total love—gaze on the cross. Easter always follows Good Friday.

We priests of the western world have very little concept of the persecution, intimidation, and repression suffered by our fellow believers in the non-Christian world.

A Coptic bishop recently spoke to a Christian group in New Jersey. He was literally terrified. If he were to say one word that could be construed as inimical to Islam, and it was carried back to Egypt, his people there could be attacked. For 1400 years, these people have lived under the heel of Muslim domination. We in the West risk nothing.

> So they left the presence of the Sanhedrin, rejoicing that they had been found worthy to suffer dishonor for the sake of the name. —Acts 5:41

> The priest is called to take Christ as his model in all his behavior. —Jean Galot, S.J.

> The priest has the power of taking hold of the very life of God, of communicating it to his brethren, of making them into sons of the Most High. —J. Perinelli, O.P.

76.

With such affection for you, we were determined to share with you not only the gospel of God, but our very selves as well. . . . —1 Thessalonians 2:8

My brother,

Have you ever been in an assignment that fit you like a glove? The people were wonderful—friendly, eager to serve the Lord, generous in their gifts to the church. There were few financial problems and few social problems. All was harmonious.

Most of all, you felt loved, appreciated, and cared for. In truth, you were near to heaven on earth. You could have stayed there for a lifetime.

Then came the change. A new assignment. By comparison, everything seemed alien—different. Perhaps the people seemed cold and hostile.

My brother, this second assignment is for you a greater opportunity—a greater challenge. Your goodness, kindness, meekness, and patience can change even hostility and indifference to love. Give generously and you shall receive—more than you can dream of.

In the 1950s, there was a hugely popular pastor. He had a great Irish parish, a high school and grammar school, three curates, and thirty-five nuns in the convent. He was a much sought after speaker. His humor and delivery were flawless. He was in heaven.

Then he was asked to go to another huge parish. It was a different ethnic makeup. It had problems. People were moving away. He inadvertently made a few humorous ethnic remarks. In the words of Queen Victoria, the people "were not amused."

Five years later, this pastor was an alcoholic, an incompetent administrator, and a most unhappy person.

Brother, you cannot let the assignment—the job—control your life. Life itself is too uncertain.

Whoever preaches, let it be with the words of God. . . .
—1 Peter 4:11

Like his master, the priest is called to carry out the work of redemption and there is no other path of salvation, no other way by which people can be saved, but by the way of the cross. —Frederico Suarez

Lay people notice the difference between a priest who seeks the glory of the Lord, and one who seeks himself.
—Aloysius Biskupek, S.V.D.

77.

I am caught between the two. I long to depart this life and be with Christ, [for] that is far better. Yet that I remain [in] the flesh is more necessary for your benefit.
—Philippians 1:23, 24

My brother,
Saint Paul had been the recipient of a mystical experience—the sensible presence of Christ. He wrote in his epistles of being drawn up into the "third heaven" (2 Cor 12:2). His entire life after conversion was a contrast of enormous stress and suffering counterbalanced by the inner radiance of the divine power that urged him on.

It is no wonder, then, that he would be torn by opposite desires. Certainly, he longed to be freed from the flesh and carried into the union with God that all the saints experience. He also realized the importance of his mission—and the need for his guiding leadership within the nascent Christian community.

My brother, there are not many who are called as Paul was. We can only pray to do the Lord's work one day at a time. The desire to lay down our ministerial burden may attract us—but our life is Christ's. Our desires do not matter.

> We have to do the works of the one who sent me while it is day. Night is coming when no one can work.
> —John 9:4

> The ministry cannot produce spiritual and saving results unless it is exercised in accord with the meaning of Christ as disclosed in the gospel, and imprinted in the depths of the priest's own being. —Jean Galot, S.J.

> We must wait for God, long, meekly, in the wind and the wet, in the thunder and the lightning, in the cold and the dark; wait and he will come. He never comes to those who do not wait. —Father Faber

The priesthood is a supreme testimony of love for Christ, which no other state or vocation can excel or even equal. —Raymond A. Tartre, S.S.S.

78.

Although I am free in regard to all, I have made myself a slave to all so as to win over as many as possible. . . . To the weak I became weak, to win over the weak. I have become all things to all, to save at least some. All this I do for the sake of the gospel, so that I too may have a share in it.
—1 Corinthians 9:19, 22, 23

My brother,

The ideal of the evangelist is to truly bring the "good news" to all people. In a certain sense, that is the easiest task. An evangelist preaches, teaches, exhorts, and inspires. Then he often moves on.

The resident servant of the servants of God has a much more difficult task. The people are truly harsh taskmasters. They expect so much from a priest. Often they ask the man of God to be their friend, consoler, problem solver, and even psychiatrist. The church is the only place where the people expect no less than another Jesus to serve as leader. In the complex life of today's society, it is physically impossible to be "all things to all men."

You, my friend, must use all the talent, ability, and wisdom that God has given you for the faithful. But you can only do what your physical strength can permit. He who tries to do too much will do too little.

Not to us, Lord, not to us
    but to your name give glory. . . .
—Psalms 115:1

Priests should be capable of transforming into practical terms theological ideas, principles, and concepts for the people. —Gustav Thils

The Christian at almost every important stage of his mortal career, finds at his side, the priest with power from God. —Pope Pius XI

Parish priesthood is inclusive . . . nothing is above us and nothing is below us because we are general practitioners. —Timothy Dolan

The normal concern of an American bishop is not about clerical complacency, or inactivity, but rather about restraining priests from working at an abnormally high pace. I might add that this is also the concern of many doctors who are asked to attend to the health of a priest. —Cardinal John J. Krol

79.

. . . that we might trust not in ourselves but in God who raises the dead. —2 Corinthians 1:9

My brother,

Saint Paul reminds you and me of the enormous power of God. His total control over life and death is a given.

Yet the ways of the Lord are mysterious. It is for mankind to trust in God, but to use all the means at humanity's command to make this world new and beautiful—a garden of Eden.

So, while we believe in God's omnipotence, and we trust in his love and care for us, the priest must forge that bond of confidence that makes God real to those around us.

No, we cannot raise the dead. Nor can we change the course of human events in every situation. Yet with God's help, all things can conspire for good. Even death itself carries lessons of hope and eternal life to those affected.

We must not let people grieve as those who have no hope, brothers. God and resurrection are real. We must transmit the vision to the eyes of those who weep.

Since Vatican Council II, the rites surrounding funerals have changed. Before, we said the Rosary for the deceased person's soul at the wake. We celebrated Mass in black to symbolize grief. The prayers at the Mass and at the grave centered upon the need to pray for the deceased. The last things—judgment, heaven, hell, or purgatory—were exceedingly real to the family and friends of the deceased.

Now, we might wonder if every funeral Mass has become a rite of canonization. If we really believe the eulogies, most of the deceased are great saints. They would inspire us to pray to the deceased, rather than for the deceased.

> As you sent me into the world, so I sent them into the world. —John 17:18

> Jesus says, "For them, I sanctify myself in truth because they too are myself. There will be one Christ, loving Himself." —St. Augustine

> To believe is to see with the eyes of God. —St. Thomas

> Oh, my soul, never forget your dead, for they live. —Karl Rahner, S.J.

80.

There is no partiality with God. —Romans 2:11

My brother,

In the Latin text, Paul is speaking of *"acceptio personarum."* *Acceptio personarum* means more than "favoritism."

Favoritism always involves two or more, one of which is accepted and blessed more than the other.

Acceptio personarum is an absolute statement. It refers to the soul of each person, in and on his own, having a special relationship with God that separates that person from the common human fate decreed by divine providence. We are not just a statistic—a number.

All men and women are accepted by the Lord in a special way. But no one, not even Jesus, was exempt from the human condition so utterly that they were given a life more angelic than human.

"Rejoice" because you are special. God knows you intimately. Everything about you is unique.

Because we share a common lot with Jesus, our special lives will have many blessings—but also we will bear its crosses.

In short, we are all human.

"Did I not choose you twelve?" —John 6:70

Cleanse me, O Lord, and purify my heart, that cleansed in the blood of the lamb, I might enjoy eternal joys.
—Prayers for Donning the Alb (Pre-Vatican Council II)

Authority does not accrue to the priest because the community appoints him. It is brought into his being by the character which lets the face of the Lord appear in him. —Jean Galot, S.J.

A healthy self-esteem has to be ultimately irrevocably rooted in God's love, climaxed in the victory in Jesus.
—George A. Aschenbrenner, S.J.

I will not try to save my soul by defacing an original painting, which has its own merits, in order to become an unsuccessful copy of someone else. —Pope John XXIII

81.

To Greeks and non-Greeks alike, to the wise and the ignorant, I am under obligation. . . . —Romans 1:14

My brother,

We have two big crosses to bear. One is to deal with our own shortcomings and faults. The other cross can be worse. It is to bear with people.

How wonderful it would be if all of our Catholics were bright, good-humored, generous, and sensitive people. What a beautiful world it could be to be able to spend our lives with people who are fun to be with and very self-sufficient; they would make life itself a joy.

But, unfortunately, life is not a walk in the park. We meet the people we like, and the people who are not pleasant. We deal with the selfish, the egotistical, the supersensitive, the boorish, and sometimes those who are just plain ignorant and who don't see anything except what they desire to see.

So consider this. As we want God to be generous to us and to forgive our faults, so must we try—and try again—to love our neighbor—including the good, the bad, and the ugly.

Father Joe DiPeri, as a seminarian, had a dry, at times penetrating, sense of humor. One day, he said to another fellow, "I have to love you. I could never like you."

They both laughed. But the other man, an obnoxious, overbearing blowhard, got the message.

> I will show you what someone is like who comes to me, listens to my words, and acts on them. —Luke 6:47

> Those who govern [in the church] must find their happiness, not in themselves, commanding men, but in being useful to them. —M.G. Bardy

> The form of humility [of the apostle] makes him absolutely available and prepared for anything. —Gustav Thils

> The priest should not approach his task with a predetermined spiritual program which he tries to superimpose upon souls, or present an ascetical straight jacket into which he tries to slot people. —Pope John Paul II

82.

Conduct yourselves wisely toward outsiders, making the most of the opportunity. Let your speech always be gracious, seasoned with salt, so that you know how you should respond to each one. —Colossians 4:5–6

My brother,

The Vulgate translates the beginning of the passage above, *"in sapientia ambulate."* "To walk in wisdom" is no easy task. It is an everyday grace for which we need to pray.

Did you ever notice that often, when you find yourself upset, angry, or disappointed, it happened without warning? In football terms, we can get "blindsided." We are going along peacefully and happily. Suddenly some stupid thing happens that we did not anticipate.

Instantly, our thyroid, pituitary, and adrenal glands go to work. We are in a state where literally we are "fit to be tied." We find ourselves reacting instinctively and saying things we never meant to utter.

That is the difference between the truly wise man—the truly holy man—and the rest of us. The holy man is always controlled and peaceful. He deals with the unforeseen with peace and serenity. It is an ideal to which we can all aspire. But it will not be easy to attain.

Some men are gifted with a calm, placid, imperturbable manner. It can be envied.

One night a fight broke out at the high school basketball game. A priest waded into the crowd, breaking up the kids. Finally, the priest had one boy pinned up against a wall. The late, great Father John Merity, passed by, arrayed in cassock, cape, and biretta. He glanced at the priest and uttered one word as he sailed off into the night. "Disgusting," was the word. The priest dropped the kid. "Someday, I'm going to murder Merity," he thought.

Set a guard, Lord, before my mouth,
a gatekeeper at my lips.
Do not let my heart incline to evil
or yield to any sin.
—Psalms 141:3–4

Humble self-knowledge is a more sure way to God than searching the depths of learning. —Thomas à Kempis

The priest must carry in himself the genuine traits of the Savior and he must let them radiate.
—Jean Galot, S.J.

Pathological emotional disorder is an over-tilting in one direction to such an extent that the plane does not tilt back again. —Thomas Vernon Moore, M.D., Carthusian

83.

So then, while we have the opportunity, let us do good to all, but especially to those who belong to the family of the faith.
—Galatians 6:10

My brother,

Again, the Vulgate has in the passage above, *"dum tempus habemus,"* or "while we have time." There is for each of us a time to be born, a time to die, a time to plant, a time to reap.

None of us can guarantee even one more day. Yet, every morning, the sun also rises on our own world of opportunity. Every day God gives us is a bonus.

So, let us use our time to "do good." It does not need to be to "all men"—only to those within our own sphere of human intercourse, the people we are assigned to serve and the people who serve within the orbit of our own activity.

The household of faith lies in our own kitchen, our own refectory, in the sacristy, the school, the parish center—and, above all, the church.

It doesn't take much to make others happy. A smile—a compliment—a blessing—a hug. Brother, there is an enormous need for someone to care because there are so many who are lonely.

There was a time when, because of a diocesan job that I held, I had to visit many rectories. Each one was different. Each reflected the men who lived there.

Some were active, noisy, happy places filled with activity. The secretaries and domestics reflected a joyous spirit.

Others were glum, quiet, and overly serious. A person could sense the tension among the staff.

Others, of course, were more formal and businesslike. People were more professional in their attitude. Some were professional, meaning also warm and courteous. Some were professional, meaning cold and impersonal.

What effect do you have on your house? How do you affect your environment?

> Above all, let your love for one another be intense, because love covers a multitude of sins. —1 Peter 4:8

> Love softens all things and makes every bitter thing sweet. —Thomas of Celano

> I joyfully realized that everything around me was a sign of God, His token, and I could no longer look at anything without thinking of Him, My Most High and Good Lord. —Carlo Carretto

> Moving from doer to animator is not achieved easily. —Brother Loughlan Sofield, S.T.

PRIEST:
A MAN FOR ALL SEASONS

84.

... on the contrary, in everything we commend ourselves as ministers of God, through much endurance, in afflictions, hardships, constraints, beatings, imprisonments, riots, labors, vigils, fasts; by purity, knowledge, patience, kindness, in a holy spirit, in unfeigned love, in truthful speech, in the power of God; with weapons of righteousness at the right and at the left; through glory and dishonor, insult and praise. We are treated as deceivers and yet are truthful; as unrecognized and yet acknowledged; as dying and behold we live; as chastised and yet not put to death; as sorrowful yet always rejoicing; as poor yet enriching many; as having nothing and yet possessing all things. —2 Corinthians 6:4–10*

My brother,

If we were faced with all of the above, not many of us would long endure.

Saint Paul lays out the struggle and suffering of himself and his companions, not to intimidate us—or impress us with their heroism. The clue lies in the last line: We seem to have nothing, yet everything is ours.

We too will undoubtedly suffer much—psychologically and sometimes physically—for the faith in our work as ambassadors of Christ to a fallen world. Sometimes, it will seem as if we have labored in vain, that our ministry is inadequate, and that our own self worth is depleted to almost nothing.

Yet, brother, you do have everything you need, for you are Christ's and Christ is God's. Your very essence is priestly. The trials of this world are as nothing. In fact, the world itself is nothing compared to the riches that God has implanted in your very being and those that lie stored up for you in heaven.

You may be like Christ on the cross, but when all else is gone, God is there. Above all, do not allow yourself to become physically or psychologically ill. You are not alone. The church needs you. The church must support you. After all, the church is Christ on earth. From the standpoint of the priesthood, we are all in this together. Make sure that you have a priest friend with whom you can share. There you will find Christ.

> I do not ask you that you take them out of the world but that you keep them from the evil one. —John 17:15

> The priest is God's possession in a more special way, not only because of a movement that links him to God, but also because of a movement whereby God Himself turns to mankind and undertakes to save it.
> —Jean Galot, S.J.

> Priests need priests, the love, understanding, respect of their fellow priests. —Father Emile Brie

> From a medical and psychiatric point of view, priesthood is indeed a high-risk occupation.
> —Father James J. Gill, S.J., M.D.

85.

[But] whatever gains I had, these I have come to consider a loss because of Christ. More than that, I even consider everything as a loss because of the supreme good of knowing Christ Jesus my Lord.—Philippians 3:7, 8

My brother,

"Sacrifice," the consecration of something by surrendering it to God, is not unknown to others. All religions know sacrifice.

But as we as Christians mature and become more at one with the One, our vision begins to change. As we grow older, certain things no longer seem as important. Material possessions can become a burden. The estimation of men seems to matter less. Even physical comforts become narrowed to a few basics.

Saint Paul considers all things as loss—actually, his phrase is much more crude; he considers all things as garbage—in the light of the knowledge of Jesus. As you know, in Paul's world, knowledge was not just an intellectual concept. It meant a shared relationship that was deep and lasting and vitalizing. As Paul fell more and more in love with the Christ, all else mattered less. So it will be for us—if we are faithful.

There was a bumper sticker on some cars in the 1990s. It read, "The guy who dies with the most toys, wins."

For those baby boomers who became the high rolling entrepreneurs of that era, that statement was more than a joke. Sadly, it was a philosophy of materialism to be lived.

We can own "things," especially if they are useful. The question is this: do they own us?

> No servant can serve two masters. He will either hate one and love the other, or be devoted to one and despise the other. —Luke 16:13

> A priest has nothing to gain and everything to lose by constant association with people of the world. —Jacques Millet, S.J.

> If a priest fails to integrate the supernatural and the human, if either of these two factors fail him, his personality will suffer as a result. —Frederico Suarez

> Everything that smacks of pretension and self-assertion is only selfishness and comes to naught. —Pope John XXIII

86.

*We know that all creation is groaning in labor pains even
until now; and not only that, but we ourselves, who have the
first fruits of the Spirit, we also groan within ourselves as we
wait for adoption, the redemption of our bodies.*
—Romans 8:22, 23

My brother,

Paul expresses the yearning and desire that all creation manifests as it waits for the *pleroma*—the fullness of time when all
things are subsumed into the perfection of the "One," the
"True," and the "Holy"—the subsistent Creator.

We ourselves have reached a degree of maturity. We have
received the plenitude of the Spirit in Baptism, Confirmation,
and Holy Orders. Yet, we are not complete.

Weighted by spiritual weakness, and even physical failures
at times, there is an instinct in us that at times wants to cry out,
"Enough, Lord. This journey tires me. I want to run to you, but
all things conspire inwardly and outwardly to restrain me."

Brother, patience is a true virtue. Be patient with your soul.
Be patient with your body. Let God do the work! He can, you
know! He will.

There are always some priests who are on a career track that
is rewarding and exciting. Scholars follow the road of intellectual pursuits. They investigate. They write books and articles.
Others enter the ranks of the diocesan hierarchy. They are busy
associating with bishops and doing important things. Some
men are great administrators and builders. They move from
project to project, from success to success.

But so many, many of us are simply "on the job,"—day by
day. We are like parents in that our greatest gift is a combination of service and presence. For us, there is a spiritual race to
run and to win. But our lives are hardly exciting. At times, life
is even dull and tedious. Yet, without us, where would the
church—Christ—be?

So you also are now in anguish. But I will see you
again, and your hearts will rejoice. . . . —John 16:22

Since the sure and only sign of true friendship is to will
the same thing (idem velle, idem nolle), we must let
that mind be in us which was in Christ Jesus.
—Pope Pius X

We look for God outside of ourselves, and all the time
He is within. —Eugene Boylan, O.C.R.

If every day is "everyday," then every day is your day,
and every hour is the hour of your grace.
—Karl Rahner, S.J.

87.

*I consider that the sufferings of this present time are as
nothing compared with the glory to be revealed for us.*
—Romans 8:18

My brother,

Paul may have been a better person than you or I in some
things. This is probably an example.

Glory, in Hebrew, belongs to God above. It is that shining
presence, and at times, that dark cloud that covered Moses on
Mount Sinai. It filled the Temple when Solomon had completed his work and it was being consecrated. Glory shone from
the Lord Jesus and from the cloud above on Mount Tabor.

But you and I have probably never had an experience such
as witnessing God's glory—the *Shekinah*. It is hard to think of
heaven when we suffer here below.

But trust in the Lord. Get through today—just today.

That glory to be revealed is a vision of hope. It can pull us in
when we are weary as a thirsty man in a desert is drawn to a
distant oasis. But God gives us today, just today. We must live
for God in this moment.

Father Charlie McTague is a legend at the age of eighty-four.
He has lived four or five lives wrapped up in one as a parish

priest, a sailor, a chaplain, and an innovator. He is the priest who first introduced the Korean community into Bergen County, New Jersey, giving them homes, finding them jobs. Every time Charlie is asked, "How are you?" his answer is invariably the same, "I'm the luckiest man on the face of the earth. I'm happy to be alive." Charlie's perennial good will and cheery attitude can be disconcerting for the priests around him. After all, everybody has to be ill-tempered sometimes. Or do they?

> Do not worry about tomorrow; tomorrow will take care of itself. Sufficient for a day is its own evil.
> —Matthew 6:34

> The merit of eternal life is not attributed so much to our own works, as to the works of Christ, our head, who performs in us and through us. —Cajetan

> Strive to please God. —Roman Pontifical

88.

> . . . all who want to live religiously in Christ Jesus will be persecuted. —2 Timothy 3:12

My brother,

Isn't this a mystery! Why does it happen so often that good, kind, generous people are rewarded with disdain—even persecution?

To understand this, we must understand that it is not just a Christian phenomenon. It lies deep within the human race itself. Probably even in the Ice Age, cave dwellers were in a situation where many good people were treated poorly by fools and losers.

The source of the problem can lie in two areas. One is jealousy. There is something in a good person that can outrage the evil person. The very presence of a happy, decent human being can cause a psychological reaction in the inadequate personality.

Secondly, the essential goodness of a moral human being is a reproach to the less moral person. His very life is a reproach to the other.

So, friend, expect the cross. There will always be someone to whom your life and lifestyle will be an irritant. Don't let others get you down. If your conscience is clear, rejoice in the Lord. The reality is that many people—even educated priests—never really mature.

One profession that few parish priests—both diocesan and religious—are involved with is academia. We are not familiar with universities.

However, if you were to be part of that world, you could be amazed at the amount of jealousy, backbiting, competition, and egomania that can be found on any university campus.

Imagine. These are reputedly the brightest scholars and the most gifted people. Yet, they often act like children. Every department of study can be a battleground of personalities.

So, my friend, understand well that intellectual ability and emotional maturity can be two very different things.

> Take my yoke upon you and learn from me, for I am meek and humble of heart. . . . —Matthew 11:29

> The whole discipline of Christian wisdom lies not in abundance of words, not in the ability of argumentation, not in a desire of praise and glory, but in the true and voluntary humility which Jesus Christ chose and taught from the womb of His Mother to the suffering of the Cross. —St. Leo

> None but the humble maintain the true dignity of human nature. —Jacques Millet, S.J.

89.

*. . . to know him and the power of his resurrection and [the]
sharing of his sufferings by being conformed to his death. . . .*
—Philippians 3:10

My brother,

This kind of talk makes one think of martyrs—witnesses to Christ, waiting in cells to be tortured and killed. It is as if we were being invited to the cross.

But that is not what Paul means. He is speaking of our "interior" death to the world and its allurements. There comes a time in the spiritual life when things that were so desirable and alluring before no longer have any hold on us.

When we are dead to them, we find enormous freedom, joy, and relief. The hero, especially the Christian hero, is a person who bears all things with equanimity. He has suffered. He has counted all as loss. Now, the hero walks through life seeing reality. He knows true value. He lives for Christ.

Strange, when we die to the world, we can enjoy it even more.

Bishop John J. Dougherty was undoubtedly one of the greatest men that the Archdiocese of Newark has ever produced. A ground-breaking scripture scholar, a renowned television and radio personality (another Fulton Sheen), a bishop, a president of a university, a United Nations delegate, John had everything—looks, brains, wit, and holiness.

But John Dougherty revealed his true greatness after he suffered a devastating stroke. When he recovered well enough to get around, his good humor and admirable demeanor impressed everyone. His laughter was contagious. And, though his body was impaired, his mind remained brilliant as ever.

Our inner essence is not what we do. It is who we are.

Take care to guard against all greed, for though one
may be rich, one's life does not consist of possessions.
—Luke 12:15

The true science of every man is of his everlasting happiness. If he knows that, he knows it all. If he is ignorant of that, he knows nothing.
—Jacques Millet, S.J.

The priesthood is essentially altruistic.
—Aloysius Biskupek, S.V.D.

90.

But, even if I am poured out as a libation upon the sacrificial service of your faith, I rejoice and share my joy with all of you. —Philippians 2:17

My brother,

Most priests are not called upon to make the ultimate sacrifice of martyrdom. Yes, there are heroes all over the world—priests, religious, and lay people—who spend their lives in hardship and danger. But the vast majority of us pour out our lives, minute by minute, hour by hour, year by year, until the hourglass runs out and our chronological time is over.

But, my friend, your life is a daily sacrifice, a daily consecration to God. Your presence on the altar and your assignment with its daily duties are marked by the call of bells and phones. Your people seek you out. They demand your time. They exact from you a service.

The morning offering of the priest is so important. It creates a focus for your day. Every prayer, work, joy, and suffering becomes a drop of your lifeblood spent in the work of God.

Brother, your whole life is a liturgy of praise to the Creator. Just recognize how precious your time is. How God loves your generosity!

Tend the flock of God in your midst, [overseeing] not by constraint but willingly, as God would have it. . . .
—1 Peter 5:2

If there is anyone who is not allowed to live his own life, that person is the priest. —Frederico Suarez

Priests cannot limit their sacrificial offering to the ritual performance of the Eucharist. They are called upon to commit themselves by making that total gift of their own selves which the Eucharist implies for their own personal lives. —Jean Galot, S.J.

A man could just sizzle to burnout because of the drudgery of so much routine and repetition conjoined with a requirement of almost infinite availability. —George A. Aschenbrenner, S.J.

91.

In your struggle against sin you have not yet resisted to the point of shedding blood. —Hebrews 12:4

My brother,

All of us are aware of the saints who fought the desires of the flesh by violent and harsh penances. Not many of us would have the courage to roll naked in the snow, or to jump into thorn bushes to calm our passion. The saints may fast and afflict their bodies in grievous ways, but that is not normal spirituality for most religious folks.

In addition, all violent penances are dangerous. Satan can use even those to cause us to fall into great sins. Neurasthenia is not helpful in living a life dedicated to God.

Yet, most of us fail at the other end. The flesh weighs us down. Even as we grow older, life can become more difficult. It is just too easy to "go with the flow." We are too tired to fight.

So, brother, a fighter needs to be in tiptop shape. Stay well! Stay healthy! And you will be more likely to serve the Lord and the church in a more perfect manner. You will be a happier person while serving.

There are many "signs" of burnout in the priesthood. When a man does not want to get up to face another day, when he begins to eat, drink, or smoke too much, when he buries himself in the television, when his Mass takes about twelve minutes, when he disappears into his room for much of the day—all of these are those signs. The problem is often this. No one cares. As long as the priest is functioning even at a minimum level, no one says anything—until he ends up in rehab, or in the hospital, or dead.

> . . . That I may come to the altar of God,
> to God, my joy, my delight.
> Then I will praise you with the harp,
> O God, my God.
> —Psalms 43:4

> There are men so burdened with cares and sorrows that like lame men, they are limping and hardly ever advancing on the road of salvation.
> —Aloysius Biskupek, S.V.D.

> In the soul of a saint, action and contemplation, blending in perfect harmony, give his life a marvelous unity. —Dom Chautard

> It is characteristic of manic patients that they do things by excess. —Thomas Vernon Moore, M.D., Carthusian

FIDELITY: ON THE JOB DAY BY DAY

For he must reign until he has put all his enemies under his feet. —1 Corinthians 15:25

My brother,

Christianity is a religion of love. We are taught to love our enemies. It is not a question of "even" loving our enemies. It is a question of "especially" loving them. "What good is it if you only love those who love you?"

But here is the problem. For us to be able to truly love our enemies, we must be able to examine ourselves first. If our conscience is pure and limpid—if we have done nothing to create an enemy by some bad deed of ours—then we can love them.

If, in reality, we have some sense of guilt, if we have wrongly provoked our adversary, then we cannot say that we "love" him or her.

However, if in our heart, we have done nothing to offend another, then with an open and honest heart, we can love them. We can feel sorry for the other, for the other bears the burden of hatred.

So the martyrs could pray for and bless their persecutors. In a strange way, we can love our adversaries more than others, for their chastisements inflicted upon us, can be seen as the hand of God that afflicts and purifies us.

Some people are difficult—almost impossible to love. In the old days, rectory life was more difficult. Three or four men were assigned to one house. The personalities were bound to be diverse. The key, of course, was the pastor. If he was a tyrant, it wasn't too bad. The brothers had a common enemy. If he delegated his authority to a "first curate," life could be hell on earth. If he exercised no authority, life could be chaos.

But, with all of the horror stories, it is remarkable how many good men served as beautiful priests of God.

> Yet it was our infirmities that he bore,
> our sufferings that he endured. . . . —Isaiah 53:4

Sincerity and kindness sum up all that one's speech should be. It makes a man Christ-like.
—Eugene Boylan, O.C.R.

But in the commandments of human superiors we find nothing but a human will, and thus, instead of making us free, they take away freedom, unless we obey them out of love of You. —Karl Rahner, S.J.

93.

Of this I became a minister by the gift of God's grace that was granted me in accord with the exercise of his power. To me, the very least of all the holy ones, this grace was given, to preach to the Gentiles the inscrutable riches of Christ, and to bring to light [for all] what is the plan of the mystery hidden from ages past in God who created all things. . . .
—Ephesians 3:7–9

My brother,

From this passage, you might believe that Saint Paul was the mildest and most meek of men.

Far from it! This is the Paul who wrote his greatest letters in a mood of anger and almost insufferable righteousness. This is the Paul who "resisted Peter to his face." This is the Paul who tells the world that he is the equal of all the apostles. This is the Paul who thunders threats on the Corinthians and others who have gone to another gospel.

Yes, he was the last of the apostles, chosen in fact by God himself. Yes, he had been a persecutor of Christians. Yes, he had to struggle with the "pillars of the church" to continue his mission in his own manner.

But, he clearly recognized his mission. His vocation was to the Gentiles. He was commissioned by God for that role.

Brother, whatever your assignment, you were commissioned for your ministry. Never doubt your place or your commission in the divine plan.

In the early days followingVatican Council II, when ecumenism was all the rage, the very first meeting ever held between Protestants and Catholics in Kearny, New Jersey, was held in a Methodist church. A very tall distinguished Anglican churchman came over to the young Catholic priest. "Father," he said in a very English accent, "what are you and I doing here with all these Protestants?"

Since that time, the young priest—now old—has had to ask himself many times the same question, "What am I doing here?"

> Then I heard the voice of the Lord saying, "Whom shall I send? Who will go for us?" "Here I am," I said, "send me!" —Isaiah 6:8

> The Lord has placed us as patterns and mirrors, not only for the faithful, but for all the world.
> —St. Francis of Assisi

> The office of pastor is not confined to the care of the faithful as individuals, but is also properly extended to the formation of a genuine Christian community.
> —Decree on the Ministry and Life of Priests

94.

Now if the ministry of death, carved in letters on stone, was so glorious that the Israelites could not look intently at the face of Moses because of its glory that was going to fade, how much more will the ministry of the Spirit be glorious? For if the ministry of condemnation was glorious, the ministry of righteousness will abound much more in glory. . . . Now the Lord is the Spirit, and where the Spirit of the Lord is, there is freedom. —2 Corinthians 3:7-9, 17

My brother,

Paul was not bashful or shy in his assessment of the Old Testament, the covenant between God and his people. He gives the old law its due. It was inaugurated in "Glory." That glory (*Kavod*) that led the Israelites out of Egypt permeated the very features of Moses and made his face shine like the sun, so that no man could look directly upon it. That glory was no less than the radiance of God.

But it was destined to fade. It was temporary. It was God's presence for a time until the full sun of justice should arise in the presence of our Lord Jesus Christ.

Now, since Pentecost, that shining presence of God reigns in our hearts. One day, it will be manifested when we shall "shine like the sun" in the Kingdom of the Father (Mt 13:43).

As of now, we dispense glory—the invisible glory of God— by word and sacrament.

No denomination in the world can begin to compare with the beauty, the dignity, or the magnificence of our Catholic liturgy. It contains within itself the power to evoke a sense of wonder among the faithful. The full ritual in song and word truly befits the "*trisagion*," the Holy, Holy, Holy of the angels in heaven.

What a shame it is to trivialize its power and beauty by simply performing the ceremony—mindlessly and irreverently.

One good priest said, "I'll know that the *parousia* is coming when I attend one funeral Mass where they do not use Eucharistic Prayer #2."

Father, the hour has come. Give glory to your son, so that your son may glorify you. . . . —John 17:1

Jesus Christ is the one and only source of grace, but priests are the necessary channels by which it carries to us. —Jacques Millet, S.J.

It is the office of clerics to assist devoutly, seriously, diligently, and purely at the Divine Sacrifice in which the Lamb of God is daily offered. —St. Robert Bellarmine

Holy Mass is at the center of my life and of every day of my life. —Pope John Paul II

95.

To each individual the manifestation of the Spirit is given for some benefit. To one is given through the Spirit the expression of wisdom; to another the expression of knowledge according to the same Spirit; to another faith by the same Spirit; to another gifts of healing by the one Spirit; to another mighty deeds; to another prophecy; to another discernment of spirits; to another varieties of tongues; to another interpretation of tongues. But one and the same Spirit produces all of these, distributing them individually to each person as he wishes. —1 Corinthians 12:7-11

My brother,

One of the great and sad mistakes of seminary life before Vatican Council II was in the very nature of the training.

A group of young men were gathered under one roof. They were, in effect, homogenized. They lived in a regimented daily routine that did not waver. They wore cassocks and regulation clothes—like the zimmara and biretta. They ate the same food. They recreated together.

Most of all, the greatest part of their intellectual life was memorization. Six days a week, page after page, they waded through Latin textbooks. Their primary task was to digest the material and then regurgitate it on exams. There was little, if any, room for questions or debate. There was just too much to learn.

As a consequence of such a life, a great many talents never came to light. A great many men simply conformed. How different today and how much opportunity for those aspiring to be priests—and for priests.

My friend, your talents are so precious. Never compare yourself to another. You are so singular and so precious. No priest is just "ordinary," or simply "adequate."

> He made me a polished arrow,
> in his quiver he hid me. —Isaiah 49:2

> Ministry means service, a service whose definitive model is to be found in the savior of mankind.
> —Jean Galot, S.J.

> All the good that Christian civilization has brought into the world, is, at least radically, due to the words and works of the Catholic priesthood. —Pope Pius XI

> Who has not met those "big" priests who look down from their superior height of privileged position upon the rest of men—lay and clerical. Everything about them takes on the aspect of a big production—big talk, big deals, and big friends. Everything is big but themselves. They patronize and condescend, but the thought that they are big fakes never enters into their heads. —Raymond A. Tartre, S.S.S.

> The ordained priest is, as it were, an icon of Christ.
> —Thomas J. McGovern

96.

Do not quench the Spirit. —1 Thessalonians 5:19

My brother,

The Spirit blows where he wills. And like the wind, we do not know his coming or going.

Yet, in our ministry, the Spirit abides. He is no transitory feeling or emotion. By Baptism, Confirmation, or Holy Orders, we are repositories of the Spirit.

By that which we do in our sacred ministry, we are dispensers of the mysteries of God—dispensers of his Spirit.

There is a need to be open to the Spirit, however, in our everyday activities. The Holy Spirit is using us as a part of the divine plan.

Instinctively, we sense his presence. We feel that we should visit this person, speak on a certain topic at the liturgy, say a kind word, go to a wake, visit a hospital, write a sermon.

Every day, in many small ways, the Spirit urges us on. He has an agenda. When we do "his thing" rather than "our thing," we are completing that agenda, which is pleasing to the Lord.

There are some things that we cannot quite quantify in life. Among them are almost subconscious psychological instincts. For example, you haven't called a friend in a long time. You know that there is someone ill—perhaps in a hospital—that you haven't visited. There is a wake of someone you know—perhaps tangentially as a relative of a priest, or an acquaintance. You arrive at a point of decision—to act on your gut feeling or forget it.

Your instinct, my friend, may be the Holy Spirit. If it is at all possible—listen to his voice.

> And [behold] I am sending the promise of my
> Father. . . . —Luke 24:49

> It only takes a moment for God to enrich you.
> —Thomas Keating

God desires to possess our hearts completely; if we do not empty it of everything other than Himself, He cannot act there, nor do there what He pleases.
—Brother Lawrence of the Resurrection

Sanctity is not a rare favor, but the common lot and duty of all. —Thomas Vernon Moore, M.D., Carthusian

97.

. . . for no one can lay a foundation other than the one that is there, namely, Jesus Christ. —1 Corinthians 3:11

My brother,

Psalm 118 says that the stone rejected by the builders has become the cornerstone. Jesus Christ is the cornerstone of that new temple not built by hands; that is, the church on earth, the mystical body of Christ.

There is a great temptation in the priesthood to set off on projects that ostensibly are designed for the glory of God, but in reality are motivated more by our own ego or need for self-fulfillment. In the church of our forefathers, many huge and beautiful churches were created. Many were the expression of a great love for God that came from priests and people. Many others were testimonies to the instinct to glorify "ego" through monuments of brick and mortar.

Likewise, many worthwhile societies, groups, and associations have been created in the church. Most were to increase the devotion of the people. However, some were the expression of a desire for honor or power on the part of the founder. Some even were formed for monetary gain.

So, we all need a reality check now and then. Whom do we serve? Are our motives always pure?

There was a time, during the idealistic days after Vatican Council II, when the social apostolate was all the rage. There were new ideas, a new vision of what Christianity should be. After all, if we were truly followers of Jesus, we would "sell what we have and give it to the poor."

A concomitant opinion that went along with the social drive was a certain disdain for the old brick-and-mortar priests. They were looked upon as men who built temples and parish plants to their own glory.

It is interesting to see now, forty years later, how many of those early firebrands and revolutionaries who had such hard words for "brick-and-mortar priests" have built—or are now building—churches.

> Happy the man who obeys me. . . .
> For he who finds me, finds life
> and wins favor from the Lord. . . . —Proverbs 8:33, 35

> Pride is the root of all vices. Pride comes before a fall.
> —Aloysius Biskupek, S.V.D.

> There are the dilettantes who are active, but in their own way, according to their own tastes and caprices, not according to the good of the church. —Gustav Thils

> It is when the priest becomes so absorbed in the success of his work that he becomes prey to what Pius XII called the "heresy of action." —Raymond A. Tartre, S.S.S.

98.

For we are the aroma of Christ for God among those who are being saved and among those who are perishing, to the latter an odor of death that leads to death, to the former an odor of life that leads to life. Who is qualified for this?
—2 Corinthians 2:15, 16

My brother,

Odor is a sense of which we seldom speak. Today, we live in a very sanitized world—at least, in the First World countries. We bathe regularly. Our clothes are washed often. We brush our teeth and use mouthwash. We use deodorant. Very few of us live on farms where animals can lend their special fragrance to the atmosphere.

But, the spiritual writers speak in allegory when they speak of the "sweet odor of sanctity," or conversely, of the stench of sin.

My friend, the priest is supposed to bring the fresh quality of goodness and joy to a very sinful world. Yes, we are not always what we should be—but God knows we try.

The world is a better place because you are there. Your life brings the fragrance of God's presence to the world.

Priests often are unaware of the power of their presence. A door opens, a priest enters the room and suddenly everything changes. A patient feels comforted, a gathering becomes more joyful, the people in the funeral parlor feel the presence of God. A quarreling couple is distracted from each other by this new mediator of peace.

The problem for us priests is this. We rarely sense what we have brought with us because we live our lives without seeing ourselves as others do.

As a pleasing odor I will accept you. . . . —Ezekiel 20:41

Holy Orders leads the priest whom it consecrates to render homage to the infinite transcendence of the Most High and to permeate this homage with filial affection. —J. Perinelli, O.P.

By making real in one's life what is "heavenly," celibacy seeks to realize the Kingdom. It is essentially oriented toward the development of the church here and now. —Jean Galot, S.J.

Take a holy pride in being called and in your own identity as other Christs. —Thomas J. McGovern

99.

. . . proclaim the word; be persistent whether it is convenient
or inconvenient; convince, reprimand, encourage through all
patience and teaching. For the time will come when people
will not tolerate sound doctrine but, following their own
desires and insatiable curiosity, will accumulate teachers and
will stop listening to the truth and will be diverted to myths.
But you, be self-possessed in all circumstances; put up with
hardship; perform the work of an evangelist; fulfill your
ministry. —2 Timothy 4:2-5

My brother,

When you were studying in the seminary, do you remember
all of those old heresies that entered the church—all the
"isms"? You may remember Arianism, Donatism, Pelagianism,
Manichaeism—those ancient deviations, and others right up to
Modernism.

It never ends. The human being is always seeking something
new—something different. There isn't a priest who hasn't, at
one time or another, found himself defending the "old time
religion" to people who have a new agenda.

Any slick preacher or propagator of philosophy can gain followers. Look at the worst—someone like Jim Jones, or even an
apparently fervent Christian like Sun Myung Moon. "Itching
ears" is a good description for those who have a desire for
innovation.

But if we stay calm and peaceful, if we are sure of our faith,
then we can quietly point to the Silent Christ. They may not listen. But at least the Lord has a mouthpiece—a representative
on earth.

Our job is to prepare our people so that they will understand
and love the church of Christ. For ourselves, dialogue is for
those who are willing to hear as well as to talk.

There is a saying that, just because you have silenced an
adversary, it doesn't mean that you have converted him.

It is absolutely, totally, and completely useless to argue with
an ideologue. Ask anyone who has tried to convince a

Mormon, a Jehovah's Witness, a Seventh-Day Adventist, or a born-again Christian.

> ". . . You know that I love you." [Jesus] said to him, "Feed my sheep." —John 21:17

> The priest must preach. —Roman Pontifical

> Nothing is so foreign to the spirit of ecumenism as a false irenecism which harms the purity of Catholic doctrine and obscures its genuine and certain meaning. —The Priest and the Third Christian Millennium

> We are more necessary than ever, because Christ is more necessary than ever. —Pope John Paul II

100.

For as I see it, God has exhibited us apostles as the last of all, like people sentenced to death, since we have become a spectacle to the world, to angels and human beings alike. We are fools on Christ's account, but you are wise in Christ; we are weak, but you are strong; you are held in honor, but we in disrepute. To this very hour we go hungry and thirsty, we are poorly clad and roughly treated, we wander about homeless and we toil, working with our own hands. When ridiculed, we bless; when persecuted, we endure; when slandered, we respond gently. We have become like the world's rubbish, the scum of all, to this very moment. —1 Corinthians 4:9–13

My brother,

This is one of Saint Paul's most bitter passages. It is pure sarcasm. He is addressing his fellow Christians. He is comparing two separate lifestyles.

Today, most of us are not going to become "spectacles to the universe." Yet there are definitely two types of priesthood, as there are two types of men.

Some are seekers of worldly honors and comforts. They enjoy the spotlight and the prestige of the priesthood. They want to be pampered with food, drinks, and the things of the "good life." These, my brother, are men destined for a faint glimpse of the beatific vision.

Others care for the apostolate. They are busy with "good works." Honor and wealth, comfort, and a "soft" assignment mean little to them. Their greatest virtue is presence. In season and out, they are attentive to the Lord's work.

Where do we stand?

There is an unspoken but real problem here. Priests in the inner city do not get a great many Mass stipends. They receive few gifts from parishioners, and in some cases, the parish can hardly pay their salaries.

Some priests refuse inner city assignments. More than that, they actually visit parishes to decide if all of the amenities that they desire are present—roomy quarters, garages with remote-controlled doors, good food, plenty of time off. One might wonder about their vision of priesthood.

> Then what did you go out to see? Someone dressed in fine clothing? Those who wear fine clothing are in royal palaces. Then why did you go out? To see a prophet?
> —Matthew 11:8, 9

> Detach yourself from creatures until you are stripped of them. For the devil has nothing of his own in this world and naked he comes to battle. If you go clothed to fight him, you will soon be pulled to the ground for he will have something to catch you by. —St. Gregory the Great

> The world today has rejected the cross, which as always is totally foreign to its way of thinking.
> —Frederico Suarez

101.

Brothers, even if a person is caught in some transgression, you who are spiritual should correct that one in a gentle spirit, looking to yourself, so that you also may not be tempted. Bear one another's burdens, and so you will fulfill the law of Christ. —Galatians 6:1, 2

My brother,
Paul knows that value of fraternal charity and mutual support.

A brother is a better defense than a strong city, and a friend is like the bars of a castle (Prv 18:19).

We all know how precarious is the life of the priest. No one can be certain of tomorrow. Since we are—each and every one of us—made of clay, we are fragile.

Priests need strong ties. A lone man walks a dark road. Perhaps a hermit can do well. But those of us who are in the marketplace of life realize that fatigue, weakness, and malaise can enter our lives.

When our brother has a problem, we all have a problem. A helping hand goes a long way. If you give a brother a lift by a word, a compliment, a smile, you have done much. The weaker he becomes, the more he needs our help.

Living with a priest who has a problem with alcohol is an experience all its own. Each day brings a new mood swing. On happy days, there is love and laughter and great good will. On "hangover" days, watch out! Any slight word can begin an argument. There can be a war over nothing. The secretaries and housekeepers have to walk on tiptoe. Wrath can come upon them at any moment. But blessed are they who bear with a man until he comes to that point when he says, "I need help." The support system means everything.

I have called you friends, because I have told you everything I have heard from my Father. —John 15:15

The pastoral ministry will have to be exercised in an ever more collegial manner. —Jean Galot, S.J.

It is because priests enjoy a profound ontological similarity that they find themselves constituted in a profound indelible and eternal unity. —Gustav Thils

Without an appropriate communitarian air in the presbyterate, loneliness can so clutch the breathing of a priest and shorten his wind that his ministry suffers. —George A. Aschenbrenner, S.J.

102.

. . . just as I try to please everyone in every way, not seeking my own benefit but that of the many, that they may be saved. —1 Corinthians 10:33

My brother,

One of the strange things that can occur in the priesthood is a form of selfishness that goes against the grain of generosity. Now, this does not refer to physical things, as much as spiritual.

Priests are generous. Every panhandler and beggar knows that. That is why they come to us.

No, it has to do with a generosity of spirit. So many people, with so many needs, and so many problems, besiege us. After a while, it is easier to begin a pattern of avoidance.

We avoid public places. We avert our eyes from people in the street. We keep moving to avoid being stuck with certain people.

Brother, Jesus went off by himself. So should we. But also like Jesus, we must return to meet the people where they are.

There is a trick that certain politicians, bishops, and men in high places use. When they are greeting people, especially in a crowd, they briefly shake hands with one person, but their eyes have already moved on to the next person. Thus, the celebrity can say that he has greeted everyone, but in reality he has given his attention to no one.

It is a "pro forma" type of cordiality that ill befits priests. Yes, at every gathering, there are going to be bores and boors. It is legitimate to escape from them. But, brother, our people deserve our attention.

> People were coming and going in great numbers, and they had no opportunity even to eat. —Mark 6:31

> The priest is not a person who can be good or bad in himself alone; his mode of living and his conduct have a consequent effect on the people. —Pope Pius X

> Surrounded by corruptions, in a world in which everything can be bought or sold, the priest must pass through utterly free of selfishness. He is in search of souls, not of money. —St. Gregory the Great

103.

. . . for I want not what is yours, but you.
—2 Corinthians 12:14

My brother,

These words should be carved on every rectory door.

Catholic priests are forced to be, not only spiritual men, but so often we are also fundraisers, and involved in the "business" of religion. Schools, rectories, churches, and convents need repairs. Teachers and staff need to be paid.

Often, people associate the priest with a constant pressure for donations. They instinctively feel that we "want" something from them.

Brother, take care to remind our Catholics, often, that the whole purpose—the whole rationale—for all that we do is ministerial. While we ask for their financial support, it is their eternal salvation that is paramount.

When a child or an animal is habitually abused, that child or animal becomes almost immune to pain. They are so accustomed to blows that they accept them. Discipline can become ineffective.

Did you ever think that the constant preaching of money from the pulpit can have the same effect? People just become numb. They endure the noise for the sake of their faith.

One pastor preached money every Sunday of the year. His collections continued to fall. Finally, he asked for another parish. I guess he was ready to wreck that one also.

It is like the young agent from the farm bureau who came to Tennessee in the 1930s. He tried to tell an old farmer about crop rotation, fertilization techniques, and other modern methods of agriculture.

"Son," said the old farmer, "I've already been through three farms before this, and you want to teach me how to farm?"

Peter said, "I have neither silver nor gold, but what I do have I give you. . . ." —Acts 3:6

God is ready to give great things when we are ready to give up everything. —Meister Eckhart

We are deeply confused if, instead of making use of human means, we actually place our trust in them. —Frederico Suarez

104.

Welcome anyone who is weak in faith, but not for disputes over opinions. —Romans 14:1

My brother,

Today we are living in an age of religious ignorance. Ever since Vatican Council II, the catechetical side of our Catholic apostolate has been weakened. Millions are "cradle Catholics," baptized but that is all.

The vast majority of people gain their beliefs from movies and television. It comes to them in "sound bites." Religion drifts in and out of soap operas, sitcoms, and made-for-TV dramas. That which people receive is distorted—refracted through a cultural filter.

So when they ring the rectory doorbell, we may instinctively react to their boldness and ignorance. But peace, brother. These are the wandering sheep of the scripture. We may not agree with them—but we must love them. A kind word can do wonders.

One of the problems for priests today is that they are fairly "ignorant" about the ignorance of the post-baby boom generations concerning the teachings of the faith. Ignorance is a lack of knowledge, and so many of our people are simply ignorant about their faith.

Because there are so many ministries, RCIA, marriage preparation, sacramental teams, catechetical people, and others, it can happen that the modern priest is separated from the people. He really has no idea of just how little true doctrine informs our people. Cultural Catholicism can be as much about myth and superstition as about our faith. It is absolutely essential for the pastor to know what is being taught in the parish. Love-love-love, joy-joy-joy is not enough. They need spiritual nourishment, not a steady diet of feel-good emotion.

For nightmares come with many cares,
and a fool's utterance with many words.
—Ecclesiastes 5:2

A minister of the word should be equally at the service of all: the lowly as well as the great, the poor as well as the rich, the ignorant as well as the learned.
—Jacques Millet, S.J.

The clerical priest wants the church to dominate the world. His strength is not in his humility, but in his pride. His weapon is not the cross, but the power of authority. —Frederico Suarez

Very little good will be achieved by ceremonies, however beautiful, or societies, however flourishing, if they are not directed towards educating people to reach Christian maturity. —Presbyterium Ordinis

Technology is no substitute for the virtues of holiness.
—Timothy Dolan

105.

... nor did we seek praise from human beings, either from
you or from others, although we were able to impose our
weight as apostles of Christ. Rather, we were gentle among
you, as a nursing mother cares for her children. . . . You
recall, brothers, our toil and drudgery. Working night and
day in order not to burden any of you, we proclaimed to you
the gospel of God. —1 Thessalonians 2:6, 7, 9

My brother,

Sometimes, we priests fantasize and romanticize our prede-
cessors in the priesthood. We hear of the great preachers, the
ascetics, the men of faith who could influence millions by their
lives.

And sometimes, our image of the past is that of a fire and
brimstone speaker who could instill fear into the faithful with
fearful messages.

Brother, that will not work in today's modern world. Our
approach needs to be like that of Saint Paul—gentle, persuasive, and patient. Remember, we can never force a conversion.
We can only prepare the ground. God it is who will cause the
seed of faith and repentance to grow.

One of our parishes had a great fire-and-brimstone preacher.
Every Sunday, you could hear descriptions of hell as if the man
had been born and raised there. Some people naturally either
voted with their feet and went to another Mass—or another
church. Most just endured it. Except for one old Irish lady. She
sat there and smiled. My mother asked her, "Doesn't he both-
er you?"

"Not at all, Mary" she answered, "I turn off me hearing aid
and I say me rosary 'til he's finished."

I announced your deed to a great assembly;
I did not restrain my lips;
you, LORD, are my witness. —Psalms 40:10

We want to stress once more the very important place
that preaching still has in the modern Catholic
apostolate. No other form of communication can take
its place—not even the press, radio, and television.
—Pope Paul VI

Of no avail is the speech of him that teaches if he
cannot show the incentive of love.
—St. Gregory the Great

The challenge of truth is, in fact, an ineluctable
challenge when confronted with the temptation to
conform, or to seek facile popularity or personal
convenience.
—The Priest and the Third Christian Millennium

106.

Are you not my work in the Lord? —1 Corinthians 9:1

My brother,

Teachers are some of the most fortunate people in the world. They begin a school year with a blank slate. By the end of the semester, knowledge has been transmitted. The student has grown in age and wisdom. The professor can actually measure the fruit of his labor.

It is not so with us. We preach. We exhort. We teach. It seems sometimes that we are whistling in the wind. Nothing seems to have changed.

But it has, brother. The entire culture can be changed, but only one soul at a time.

Be grateful for the good that you do see in the family of God you serve. You are not preserving it. You are causing it to grow.

In the old days, it was a lot harder to preach. Consider, we had one hour to get the crowd in and out of Mass. There were no bulletins. We had to read off the banns of marriage, and the intentions for every Mass that week, plus the announcements. Also, one priest would give the sermon at every Mass. We took turns. There were times when we sounded like tobacco auctioneers.

On top of that, we priests poured out on the altar just after the consecration to give communion to hordes of kneeling souls. At the end of Mass, we had about five prayers for peace.

The point is this. There is no excuse for a bad sermon today. Priests have time and the opportunity to make the liturgy meaningful.

> [The Levites . . . explained the law to the people, who remained in their places]. Ezra read plainly from the book of the law of God, interpreting it so that all could understand what was read. —Nehemiah 8:7, 8

The most sacred task of theology is not the invention of new dogmatic formulas to replace the old ones, but rather a defense and explanation of the formulas adopted by the councils as may demonstrate that divine revelation is the source of the truths communicated through these expressions. —Pope Paul VI

Knowledge of God elevates the soul. Knowledge of self keeps it humble. —John Nicholas Grou, S.J.

Evasions of duty are self-seeking reactions rooted in human selfishness.
—Thomas Vernon Moore, M.D., Carthusian

107.

For what is our hope or joy or crown to boast of in the presence of our Lord Jesus at his coming if not you yourselves? For you are our glory and joy.
—1 Thessalonians 2:19–20

My brother,

Paul could be speaking directly to your heart. Are you not the hope of the church? Are you not the crown of those who formed you? Are you not the boast of your family, your friends, your seminary professors?

It is opportune for you to reflect on the joy you have brought to others. Every priest is a gift to the world, to the church, and especially to those who have helped to bring him to the altar.

Never doubt your worth. Your life is more precious than spun gold.

It can easily happen that a priest after years in God's service begins to have some doubt in himself—in his usefulness in society—in his very mission. That is because our worth cannot be measured in physical terms.

Once a priest was invited to an economic summit. There were many important people present. There were state, county, and local politicians who were in charge of great plans and finances. There were industrialists. There were architects and builders. There were people who controlled transportation—especially railroads, and ships, and trucks.

The priest felt intimidated. He felt that he had been invited out of courtesy.

Finally, he said to the organizer of the event, "I don't know what I am doing here." And the elected official looked directly at the priest and said, "I hope that you are saving souls. All of us need your inspiration and guidance."

> You are my witnesses, says the Lord,
> my servants whom I have chosen
> To know and believe in me
> and understand that it is I. —Isaiah 43:10

> The priest is a priest no matter in what endeavor he happens to engage—secular activities included.
> —Jean Galot, S.J.

> He who lives well is the best preacher.
> —Miguel de Cervantes, Don Quixote

> Our priestly life, like every other form of Christian existence, is a succession of responses to God who calls.
> —Pope John Paul II

108.

For we write you nothing but what you can read and understand, and I hope that you will understand completely, as you have come to understand us partially, that we are your boast as you also are ours, on the day of [our] Lord Jesus.
—2 Corinthians 1:13–14

My brother,

The priesthood is by nature a lonely life. We are surrounded by people. As in that famous statement, "We are part of every family, yet a member of none." Immersed in our assignment, we give of ourselves to any and all who ask, yet we cannot become fully joined to anyone psychologically or physically.

Saint Paul is using Greek, yet he is a Hebrew. And "to know" for a Jewish person involves not just a cognitive recognition, but in some sort of an emotional way, it has as much to do with the heart as with the mind.

In our ministerial service, there is bound to be, if we are faithful, bonds of love and affection that spring up between the man of God and his people. It is possible to "love in Christ," even more effectively than in human terms. But it may take time.

Be patient with your people, oh priest. Little by little, as they come to recognize your service, so will they come to recognize you—in love. Then they will truly be your glory.

A great preacher of missions and retreats once came to our parish. He filled the church for the week.

At the end of the mission, he said this. "I thank you for your presence. I have come to know you this week. But I must tell you this.

"I spent seven days with you, but your pastor and your priests truly know you. They know your hearts, your minds, your troubles, and your joys. Next week, I will be gone. But their love and service will still be here for you." The entire congregation applauded.

> I pray . . . that they may all be one, as you, Father, are in me and I in you, that they also may be in us, that the world may believe that you sent me. And I have given them the glory you gave me, so that they may be one, as we are one. . . . —John 17:20–22

The pastor must be a true spiritual leader, one who is concerned, alert, and sensitive to needs, one who listens seriously.
—Bishops' Committee for Priestly Life and Ministry

Lack of charity is the greatest of all heresies.
—St. Augustine

> Priestly garb is never an obstacle to the kind of
> friendship which the priest can, and needs to, have
> withthose souls trusted to his care.
> —Thomas J. McGovern

109.

Therefore, my brothers, whom I love and long for, my joy and
crown, in this way stand firm in the Lord, beloved.
—Philippians 4:1

My brother,

Here we have the same theme repeated, but with another emphasis.

Saint Paul beseeches those whom he has left behind to stand firm in the Lord.

The priest is in general a mobile servant. Therefore, he can pour his heart out and can pour his sweat into the creation of a community. Then suddenly, ripped away by a transfer, he no longer can control what happens in his former community.

Is there anything more sorrowful than to hear that all that you have created has been torn down by your successor? That where you left a flourishing community, there is now friction and trouble and even some dissolution?

There are two things to do. The first is to encourage those left behind to work for the common good. The second is this. Let go, brother! Let go! The Lord is still in charge. He has the care for his people.

There is one aspect of the Catholic parish that is most distressing. It has to do with a change in administration.

Pastors are still, in some way, potentates. As in the scripture, he can say to one "go" and he goes, and to another "come" and he comes. The lay staff, from cook, to housekeeper, to secretary, to janitor, and all the paid professionals are dispensable. A new pastor can fire them.

Most pastors are sensitive. But there are those who love to exert power. They should remember that Jesus loves the little people.

> The LORD is my light and my salvation,
> whom do I fear? —Psalms 27:1

The priest administers the sacraments but it is Jesus Christ who, by His hand, unseals the fountain of grace and with it floods the souls of the faithful.
—Jacques Millet, S.J.

The true measure of strength of personality is the power to do good.
—Thomas Vernon Moore, M.D., Carthusian

Clerics become, not despots over their people, but servants. —Raymond A. Tartre, S.S.S.

110.

Therefore, from the day we heard this, we do not cease praying for you and asking that you may be filled with the knowledge of his will through all spiritual wisdom and understanding to live in a manner worthy of the Lord, so as to be fully pleasing, in every good work bearing fruit and growing in the knowledge of God. . . . —Colossians 1:9–10

My brother,

There is a certain situation that is common to priests. It arises after they have served the Lord for a long time.

People constantly ask us to pray for them, for their people, for their troubles. Then we very easily assure them of our prayers.

That often means we make some general intention to put them in the Mass. But we "personally" do not in fact kneel before the Lord and place their needs in his hands.

Paul says that he prays "unceasingly." The difference between Paul and us is precisely here. Paul does not just make some general intention—or put someone in the prayer of the faithful. Paul actually beseeches the Lord on their behalf.

Brother, you are a pontifex, a bridge builder between man and God. The hard work of prayer must in fact be a reality in our lives.

One of the great advantages of Eucharistic Prayer #1 is that there is a place there in the old Roman Canon to pause and pray—once for the living, and once for the dead. Of course, at each Mass, there is also the Prayer of the Faithful.

It is my experience, however, that the Prayer of the Faithful has become a ritual. The general intercessions are read along with the Mass intention and then we move on. Priest, if ever on God's earth your prayers are powerful, it is at the liturgy. Treasure your intentions.

> The fervent prayer of a righteous person is very powerful. —James 5:16

> If you don't deny yourself, you will never be the soul of prayer. —The Way

> The inner life draws the blessings of God.
> —Dom Chautard

> Priests are in a very real sense an extension of Christ's Sacred Humanity. —Thomas J. McGovern

THE HOMILY:
THE MOST DIFFICULT TASK OF ALL

111.

If I preach the gospel, this is no reason for me to boast, for an obligation has been imposed on me, and woe to me if I do not preach it! —1 Corinthians 9:16

My brother,

Who among us has not dragged ourselves out of bed on a Sunday morning when we did not feel well, and then realized that we were totally unprepared to preach the good news?

There are days when we are physically ill. There are days when our own lives are in turmoil or when we are weighed down by personal problems, sadness, or just plain boredom.

When we approach the altar, there they sit—the faithful. Like little birds waiting to be fed spiritual food. It can happen at times that we almost resent them. They sit. They wait. They do nothing. They want to hear the gospel in a way that is meaningful in their lives. Not many of them realize the work that can be involved in creating a good sermon. In reality, most don't care—as long as we are short and have a point or two to give.

Brother, you get out what you put in. Continue your study of God's word and the Word will carry you even on days when you can hardly carry the word.

. . . we proclaim Christ crucified. . . . —1 Corinthians 1:23

Priests, as co-workers with their bishops, have as their primary duty the proclamation of the gospel to all.
—Decree on the Ministry and Life of Priests

The Christ preacher preaches faith. But the grace of the priesthood will work not so much by giving us eloquence as by giving our hearts illumination.
—Eugene Boylan, O.C.R.

Of all sermons, whether delivered in town or country, to peasants or men of letters, the very worst is one that is long, and heavy, and tiresome. —Jacques Millet, S.J.

Effective preaching is another fruit of personal prayer. Such preaching is effective . . . because it comes from a prayerful, sincere heart which is aware that sacred ministers are bound not to impart their own wisdom, but the Word of God, and ceaselessly invite all to conversion and holiness.
—The Priest and the Third Christian Millennium

112.

For since in the wisdom of God the world did not come to know God through wisdom, it was the will of God through the foolishness of the proclamation to save those who have faith. For Jews demand signs and Greeks look for wisdom, but we proclaim Christ crucified, a stumbling block to Jews and foolishness to Gentiles. —1 Corinthians 1:21–23

My brother,

Worldly wisdom is to be respected. It comes from a philosophical point of view that is rooted in an exaggerated regard for human freedom. We cannot take, for example, the sons and daughters of the Enlightenment with a grain of salt. They have, as a matter of fact, a better argument than we have if we begin from their premise that the human race is the beginning and end of all things.

Their premise is that the world was made for man. Each human has the right to use the world for his own benefit and enjoy every pleasure with no regret.

The cross stands alone as a reproach to the humanistic point of view. It points to God and true value.

My brother, make no mistake. You are truly a "fool" in the eyes of the world. So was Jesus.

The test of time is the true test of wisdom.

In 1931, in the encyclical *Castii connubii*, the Holy Father warned the world about the danger to the family that comes from divorce, birth control, cohabitation, abortion and other things. The world reacted with scorn and anger.

Now, consider Europe! Not one nation has a birth rate to support the nation. The older people are beginning to outnumber the young. Their national heritage is being diminished. Waves of immigrants are moving in. We are witnessing demographic suicide. No one is laughing now.

> But you, beloved, build yourselves up in your most holy faith; pray in the holy Spirit. —Jude 20

> If a pastor is to bring men to accept his ideas, he himself must be thoroughly convinced of their truth. —Jacques Millet, S.J.

> The priest is bound to be an embarrassment if he upsets the superficial calm and inert nonchalance of people who have put their soul to sleep. —Frederico Suarez

> Priests should use all modern means as aids to their ministry of salvation. —Raymond A. Tartre, S.S.S.

113.

But how can they call on him in whom they have not believed? And how can they believe in him of whom they have not heard? And how can they hear without someone to preach? And how can people preach unless they are sent? As it is written, "How beautiful are the feet of those who bring [the] good news!" . . . Thus faith comes from what is heard, and what is heard comes through the word of Christ.
—Romans 10:14, 15, 17

My brother,

It is a sure bet that you never thought of your footsteps as beautiful.

In these words, Paul has captured the essence of our task. It is to make a rational presentation of the truths of our faith.

How crippled our people have become because of the misguided efforts of some priests after Vatican Council II to "update" the faith. Many priests threw out the baby with the bath water.

They became so intent on preaching love and urging social justice that they neglected the faith which produces true charity and true social justice.

The catechism can be a bore. Yet so can scripture when it is passed mindlessly without explanation or theology. An uneducated laity is prone to error and exposed easily to false doctrine. Preach the word—all of the word.

Granted, the old catechism with its 499 questions was dull. Granted that the method of rote memory is a poor way to instruct children in the doctrine of the faith. Granted that not many were able to get past the first few questions, for example, "Who made the world?" and "Why did God make you?" Nevertheless, the proof of the effectiveness is in the results. Millions upon millions of excellent Catholics trained in the catechism had a basic grasp of the faith. Now, oh priest, if the faithful in your parish are ignorant—your work lies before you.

But they will not follow a stranger. . . . —John 10:5

Priests, therefore, constitute a section of the people of God to whom the church has entrusted an extremely important and exceptionally difficult task, namely to transform the world by transforming men.
—Frederico Suarez

Preserve inviolate and spotless the talent of the Catholic faith. You have received gold; deliver gold with lead. Teach the same things that you have learned. Though you may say things in a new way, do not say new things. —St. Vincent of Lerins

New evangelization . . . requires a genuine intellectual charity through continuous patient catechesis on the fundamentals of the Catholic faith and morals and on their influence on the spiritual life. Christian instruction is foremost among the spiritual works of mercy.
—The Priest and the Third Christian Millennium

114.

. . . that is how we speak, not as trying to please human beings, but rather God, who judges our hearts.
—1 Thessalonians 2:4

My brother,

When you stand in the pulpit, you represent Christ. You are his vicar, his ambassador.

Prudence should be your guide and truth a lamp unto your feet. The Holy Father, and the bishops, are constantly aware that their remarks will be published, scrutinized, analyzed, and finally, judged. They are most cautious and careful when they speak.

Often, the average parish priest does not realize that what he says on Sunday becomes a subject for conversation in the beauty parlor or local restaurant during the week.

If our words are guided by the truth of our faith and in a manner that is serious, yet easy to understand, our words are seeds flung out. Many of them will fall on fertile soil for the edification of the faithful.

Reflect on the precepts of the Lord,
let his commandments be your constant meditation;
Then he will enlighten your mind,
and the wisdom you desire he will grant. —Sirach 6:37

The truth assumes different names; in the schools, it is
called science, in speech veracity, in conduct frankness,
in conversation sincerity, in business honesty, in giving
advice freedom from prejudice, in keeping of promises
loyalty, and in the courts of law, it has the noble title
justice. —Father Paolo Segneri

A priest is ordained to be the defender of the truth.
—Jacques Millet, S.J.

Christianity not only comforts the afflicted but afflicts
the comfortable. —G.K. Chesterton

The human key to effective preaching of the Word is to
be found in the professionalism of the preacher who
knows what he wants to say and who is always backed
up by serious remote and proximate preparation.
—Cardinal Ratzinger

115.

*. . . but in the church I would rather speak five words with
my mind, so as to instruct others also, than ten thousand
words in a tongue.* —1 Corinthians 14:19

My brother,
   In Paul's time, ecstatic utterances were not unknown. The
charisms of the spirit were obviously present. But it is important to remember that, on Pentecost, the Holy Spirit created a
miracle of understanding—not mystery. Each apostle spoke in
his own tongue, yet the hearers heard and clearly understood
the speech of the apostles in their own language.

My brother, let your sermon be short, fervent, and above all, clear. That will please God and be more effective than mysterious utterings or babbling in an ecstatic trance.

Ecstasy has its place. However, long fasts or long hours with no sleep or intense psychological pressures can cause not holiness, but neurasthenia.

In the late 1960s and through the 1970s, the charismatic renewal swept over the American church like a wave. Many groups sprang up wherein there were *glossalalia* (speaking in tongues), prophecy, cures, phenomena such as being "slain in the Spirit," and ecstasies.

Many of our priest friends were caught up in the movement. For those involved, it was the "Holy Spirit" working in the church. For many others, it seemed more like mass hysteria.

It ended with both good and bad results.

The good can be found in the quiet, deep spirituality of a place like Steubenville University. The bad can be found among the thousands of Catholics who are now Pentecostals. As the Jesuit preacher said, "I'm not criticizing, I'm only analyzing."

To whomever I send you, you shall go;
whatever I command you, you shall speak.
—Jeremiah 1:7

A preacher says good things and says them well.
—Jacques Millet, S.J.

The proclamation of the gospel is a priestly worship
and the gift of his life a priestly sacrifice.
—Jean Galot, S.J.

When I pray, my mouth does the speaking and, if I am
praying "well," my thoughts and will-acts obediently
play their required, well-memorized little role. But is it I
myself who constitute the object of the prayer?
—Karl Rahner, S.J.

116.

For we do not preach ourselves but Jesus Christ as Lord, and ourselves as your slaves for the sake of Jesus.
—2 Corinthians 4:5

My brother,

Here Saint Paul can hit us where it hurts. How many of us go on an ego trip when we hit the pulpit?

One pastor told his associate, "Do the world a favor. Resign the papacy."

Do I preach the gospel of Christ or the gospel according to me? Do I tell people not only what Christ said, but what he meant, or what I think he meant?

There are many—priests, politicians, and others—for whom the microphone holds a fatal fascination. There are many who love to hear the sound of their own voice.

Have you ever been at a liturgy where the homilist goes on for forty minutes and then comes down from the pulpit absolutely filled with satisfaction at his sermon? Later, the priests in the sacristy groan inwardly when one well-meaning glad-hander goes to the homilist to say, "Great sermon. Wonderful." If looks could kill, the well-wisher and the homilist would both be dead.

So, my brother, one of the points in our particular examination of conscience should be this, "Do I love preaching because it makes me feel important? Am I preaching Christ or myself?"

They are waterless clouds blown about by winds. . . .
—Jude 12

The new priesthood is not characterized then by the severity of the judgment meted out on sinful mankind, but by the availability of salvation. —Jean Galot, S.J.

Egotism narrows the heart, and dwarfs and paralyzes the power of the soul. —Jacques Millet, S.J.

The preaching of priests is not a mere exercise of the word that answers to a personal need to express oneself and to communicate one's own thought, nor can it consist solely in sharing one's personal experience.
—Pope John Paul II

117.

Indeed, the word of God is living and effective, sharper than any two-edged sword, penetrating even between soul and spirit, joints and marrow, and able to discern reflections and thoughts of the heart. —Hebrews 4:12

My brother,

Saint Paul is always depicted with the scripture and a sword. If you study the lives of the saints, it is remarkable to see how many of them had an epiphany—a moment of understanding that came from the scriptures and changed their lives.

Saint Francis, Saint Ignatius, Saint Augustine and countless others were viscerally moved by either reading or hearing God's word. It can penetrate to the very inner part of the soul and cut us spiritually to the quick.

Unfortunately, many of us have become jaded over the years. Our ears and hearts are hardened. We hear—but we do not hear.

Open your heart, dear brother. If today you hear his voice, harden not your heart.

One of the ways to "hear" the scripture is to pay attention to the hymns, psalms, and reading of the daily office. We read those psalms over and over. If we only find one meaningful verse each day, we will have "heard God's voice," and in time God's word will take root in our heart. We will "enter into his rest."

I will ponder your precepts
and consider your paths. —Psalms 119:15

Many fail at mental prayer because they are trying to make a fire without fuel. They have given up spiritual reading. —Eugene Boylan, O.C.R.

Somewhat dramatically expressed, the priest has to be a living contemplation of the Word, and not simply a cultic technician or manager. —Cardinal Ratzinger

There is as little chance of living spiritually without reading as there is of living corporally without eating. —Eugene Boylan, O.C.R.

118.

When I came to you, brothers, proclaiming the mystery of God, I did not come with sublimity of words or of wisdom. For I resolved to know nothing while I was with you except Jesus Christ, and him crucified. —1 Corinthians 2:1, 2

My brother,

A good preacher constantly expands his stock of stories, anecdotes, and examples in order to get across the message. The message is the "good news" of Jesus Christ.

There are extremes. One priest decides to become a great orator. He works at developing style and delivery. He fills his sermons with all sorts of dramatic devices to hold the attention of the crowd. The danger is this. He may not be preaching Jesus—but rather preaching his own rhetoric.

The other is the priest who on the way from the sacristy to the altar asks the lector, "What's the gospel today?" Unprepared—or ill-prepared—he falls back on clichés and oft-repeated stories. Even worse, he may regale the congregation with the events of his personal life.

The media may be the message for the world. It is not for us. All of our efforts must be to one end—that Jesus Christ be better known and loved.

Cursed be he who does the Lord's work remissly. . . . —Jeremiah 48:10

Lay people notice the difference between a priest who seeks the glory of the Lord and one who seeks himself. —Aloysius Biskupek, S.V.D.

May you thus build up by word and example the house that is the family of God. —Roman Pontifical

We live in an information era characterized by rapid communication. We frequently hear experts and specialists on the television and radio. In a sense, the priest (who is also a social communicator) has to compete with these when he preaches to the faithful. Hence, his message must be presented in an attractive manner. His apostolic spirit should move him to acquire competence in the "new pulpits" provided by modern communications. —The Priest and the Third Christian Millennium

---

119.

But may I never boast except in the cross of our Lord Jesus Christ, through which the world has been crucified to me, and I to the world. —Galatians 6:14

My brother,

The cross is the symbol of pain, rejection, and humiliation. It is Christ's cross that we are to preach—not our own.

How difficult it is to bear sickness, injury, pain, or humiliation. Yet, what merit is there if we accost everyone we meet and pour out our story of woe? People will soon avoid us. Some will be charitable and listen. Some will find an excuse to cut us short.

The most difficult task is to bear our cross—silently. Our complaints and tales of sorrow may be useful to us, but they can be burdens to others when we impose our personal problems upon them.

Obviously, if we are ill or in pain, we need to go to a doctor. If we are psychologically or socially damaged, we may need professional help.

But, brother, resist the temptation to place your burden on another person's shoulders. It is Christ's cross we preach.

Some people are so locked in their own little world that they can't reach out to others.

Bishop Dougherty was fond of telling the story about the author who was absolutely in love with himself.

He collared one person and spoke for an hour about his latest book.

Then he paused and said to the hapless listener, "Enough about me now! How about you? How did you like my latest book?"

> Woe to craven hearts and drooping hands, . . .
> Woe to the faint of heart who trust not,
> who therefore will have no shelter! —Sirach 2:12–13

> How beautiful and ennobling to share the toils and fatigues of the Savior. —Jacques Millet, S.J.

> It is He whom I seek, this Jesus, who died for us. It is He whom I want, this Jesus who rose again for us. —St. Ignatius of Antioch

> Fortitude demands a certain stability of mind. —Thomas Vernon Moore, M.D., Carthusian

> When it is right to speak, I will make a point of never speaking about myself, either well or ill, and never in any way referring to my own affairs unless I am asked about them. —Pope John XXIII

120.

. . . and my message and my proclamation were not with persuasive [words of] wisdom, but with a demonstration of spirit and power, so that your faith might rest not on human wisdom but on the power of God. —1 Corinthians 2:4, 5

My brother,

We are truly fools for Christ. By that we mean fools in the eyes of the world. We are, by nature, countercultural. Our values cannot come from worldly "wisdom" nor can our message rest on human philosophers.

Faith comes from a free assent to God's word. Once we have embraced the faith, then our eyes are open to see more clearly truth and reality. Truth will always find itself in harmony with faith if faith and truth are from God.

Faith is the light that shines on dark places. It reveals that which is true. It also reveals that which is defective and false.

We must stand apart from the world and examine all things in the glow of faith and reason. That is where the power of God—like a beacon—shines on what is real and makes it evident.

You belong to what is below, I belong to what is above. You belong to this world, but I do not belong to this world. —John 8:23

Priests cannot be ministers of Christ unless they are witnesses and dispensers of a life other than this one. But they cannot be of service to men if they remain strangers to the life and conditions of men.
—Decree on the Ministry and Life of Priests

The priest must either acquire a certain level of human culture or resign himself to being enclosed in an ivory tower and being unable to relate to the mentality of the people he is supposed to bring nearer to God.
—Frederico Suarez

The modern world, to a large extent, has lost sight of man's supernatural destiny.
—Thomas Vernon Moore, M.D., Carthusian

121.

But we hold this treasure in earthen vessels, that the surpassing power may be of God and not from us. We are afflicted in every way, but not constrained; perplexed, but not driven to despair; persecuted, but not abandoned; struck down, but not destroyed. . . . —2 Corinthians 4:7–9

My brother,

What a profound thought this is! We possess a treasure—our faith. We carry it within ourselves—earthen vessels.

We are finite, mortal, and created from dust. Yet, how marvelously we are made.

Earthen vessels are truly clay—easily broken. Yet the power of God—this faith of ours—supports us.

How could the martyrs of yesterday and today bear the sufferings and persecution, the agony and pain of torture, even death itself, without some force or power that enabled them to conquer.

Surely most of them would break if left on their own strength. Yet faith gives them courage. Trust enables them to remain faithful. The earthen vessel may break. They won't.

> God indeed is my savior;
> I am confident and unafraid.
> My strength and my courage is the Lord,
> and he has been my savior. —Isaiah 12:2

We shall not likely have the good fortune, like the early apostles, to shed our blood for the salvation of our brethren, but we can and should be martyrs in spirit.
—Jacques Millet, S.J.

Martyrs die only once for Jesus Christ, while the pastor of souls must die daily for his flock.
—St. John Chrysostom

The priest must be a believer, one who converses with God. —Cardinal Ratzinger

The Laity:
Our Cross and Our Crown

122.

I give thanks to my God at every remembrance of you,
praying always with joy in my every prayer for all of you,
because of your partnership for the gospel from the first day
until now. I am confident of this, that the one who began a
good work in you will continue to complete it until the day of
Christ Jesus. It is right that I should think this way about all
of you, because I hold you in my heart, you who are all
partners with me in grace, both in my imprisonment and in
the defense and confirmation of the gospel.
—Philippians 1:3–7

My brother,

A cheerful heart is the sign of a good Christian. Time and time again, Paul uses the term "rejoice."

Yet, if we study his life, it was certainly not joyful in human terms. Consider his physical sufferings. See how much controversy fills his letters! He has trouble not only from the outside—Gentiles—but constant controversy in the very churches that he founded. There were disagreements with other apostles and evangelists.

Yet again and again, in the midst of it all, he gives thanks to God and rejoices in all of the good people and all of the good events of his life.

One of the problems of the written word is that it usually only communicates a message—not the life situation of the writer. If you only read the scriptures, would you ever believe that Jesus smiled, or that Paul laughed or that it might have been fun to be an apostle?

To follow Paul requires a joyful heart that overcomes daily problems.

The community of believers was of one heart
and mind. . . . —Acts 4:32

The priest must build a bridge between men, not a barrier. —Eugene Boylan, O.C.R.

The good pastor knows where his parish stands, what has succeeded and why, what has failed and why.

The priest is not a private practitioner. He is not a lone ranger who works in isolation.
—Father Stephen Rossetti, Ph.D.

Priests should regard themselves as living signs and bearers of the mercy which they offer, not as though it were their own, but as a free gift from God.
—The Priest and the Third Christian Millennium

123.

Yes, and I ask you also, my true yokemate, to help them, for they have struggled at my side in promoting the gospel, along with Clement and my other co-workers, whose names are in the book of life. —Philippians 4:3

My brother,

Priests are men chosen from among people to serve the community. They are all ours to serve.

Yet, is it not a truth that almost all priests find that there is a certain group around them that sustains, supports, and aids them? No priest is an island.

It is not wrong to acknowledge those who care for us. It can only be a problem if we become dependent on a certain few to the exclusion of others.

But we must bless the Lord at all times for those holy men and women who love God and are drawn to aid us in our work because of God.

Paul had a large coterie of fellow Christians—bishops, priests, men, and women who were his hands and feet. He praised God for them. Should we not thank God for those whom God has sent into our lives?

> Every day they devoted themselves to meeting together in the temple area and to breaking bread in their homes. They ate their meals with exultation and sincerity of heart, praising God and enjoying favor with all the people. And every day the Lord added to their number those who were being saved. —Acts 2:46, 47

> Community life and life in groups provide a more normal framework for priestly life and for the celibate way of life. —Jean Galot, S.J.

> Holiness is the infinite capacity to love. Only God is truly holy, because only God is infinite. But I am called to grow in holiness, to grow in the capacity to love others and to receive their love. —Robert Faricy, S.J.

> Models for shared ministry are found in Paul's letters to the Corinthians, with their theology of the body of Christ. Lay ecclesiastical ministry, flowing in its present form from the Second Vatican Council, is grounded in an image as ancient as that of the hierarchy.
> —James D. Whitehead

124.

But let our people, too, learn to devote themselves to good works to supply urgent needs, so that they may not be unproductive. —Titus 3:14

My brother,

This is an admonition to some who would prefer to hang on to the church, rather than to live their lives at hard labor.

There are many people now who look to the church for a livelihood. There are all sorts of ministries, and all sorts of paid positions.

As difficult as it is, brothers, we must deal with hard reality. There was an expression in the communist world that said, "To each according to his need; from each according to his ability."

We must care for those who labor in the vineyard of the Lord with us. We need to support and encourage them.

But there will be that most difficult moment when we must—for the good of the community—release someone from the service of the local church. Have no fear to act. Paul had the same problem.

There is absolutely no question about it. Priests are generally good guys. They are grounded in the model of Jesus. They are generous and charitable.

But as pastors and administrators, they must also be business people. Every pastor, if he is on the job long enough, will have to deal with the lazy, no-account janitor who does not do his job, with the light-fingered person who counts money on Sunday, or who works bingo, or who is an usher, with the incompetent secretary, the young person who answers the phone but who spends more time talking to her friends, the temperamental musician, or the disorganized DRE. There are times when the priest must act. But he must act prudently and with charity.

. . . but he would withdraw to deserted places to pray. —Luke 5:16

The priest's behavior towards the people entrusted to his care, whoever they are, is also a way of preparing for Holy Communion. —Frederico Suarez

When parish administration leaves much to be desired, when contact with the parishioners is broken, the work of the Lord is less easily accomplished. —Gustav Thils

125.

Only, conduct yourselves in a way worthy of the gospel of Christ, so that, whether I come and see you or am absent, I may hear news of you, that you are standing firm in one spirit, with one mind struggling together for the faith of the gospel. . . . —Philippians 1:27

My brother,

Saint Paul is describing what in the business world is called leadership. A man of conviction stands firm. He is true to his cause. Our cause is Christ.

Then, the true leader aligns himself according to his beliefs and then joins himself to the army of fellow believers.

And in unity of spirit, they "exert" themselves in one accord. In our case, it is for the gospel. He who stands firm in Christ and uses his energy for the cause of Christ will not only have an effect. His resolve and strength will lead others to make a common effort.

Amen, I say to you, whatever you bind on earth shall be bound in heaven, and whatever you loose on earth shall be loosed in heaven. —Matthew 18:18

As a total commitment to sacrifice, the mission of a shepherd cannot possibly co-exist in the exercise of a power that seeks its own advantage. Power over the flock is exercised only as dedication. —Jean Galot, S.J.

If your heart is upright, every living creature will be a mirror and a book of holy devotion. —Thomas à Kempis

Priests should preside in such a way that they seek the things of Jesus Christ, not the things that are their own. —Raymond A. Tartre, S.S.S.

Priests must sincerely acknowledge and promote the dignity of the laity and the role which is proper to them in the mission of the church. —Raymond A. Tartre, S.S.S.

126.

I urge you, brothers—you know that the household of Stephanas is the firstfruits of Achaia and that they have devoted themselves to the service of the holy ones—be subordinate to such people and to everyone who works and toils with them. I rejoice in the arrival of Stephanas, Fortunatus, and Achaicus, because they made up for your absence, for they refreshed my spirit as well as yours. So give recognition to such people.

The churches of Asia send you greetings. Aquila and Prisca together with the church at their house send you many greetings in the Lord. —1 Corinthians 16:15-19

My brother,

The church of Saint Paul was a very human institution. It was a family of believers who loved and supported each other.

In today's world, no priest can be "all things to all men" as Paul tried to do. We need the Christian family around us. All sorts of ministries are critical to a healthy Christian community.

We must recognize the worth of our parishioners and search among them for their gifts. When a priest has built the family of God in all of its parts, he has literally built up the living body of Christ and helped to form the new Jerusalem.

The just shall flourish like the palm tree,
shall grow like a cedar of Lebanon.
Planted in the house of the Lord,
they shall flourish in the courts of our God.
—Psalms 92:13-14

The roots of sanctity are planted in the depths of human frailty. —Leonardo Boff

The Christian of tomorrow will be a mystic, one who has experienced something, or he will be nothing.
—Karl Rahner, S.J.

They [the priests] should listen to the laity willingly, consider their wishes in a fraternal spirit, and recognize their experience and competence in the different areas of human activity. —Raymond A. Tartre, S.S.S.

127.

With regard to Epaphroditus, my brother and co-worker and fellow soldier, your messenger and minister in my need, I consider it necessary to send him to you. —Philippians 2:25

My brother,

See how generous Paul is. He is more concerned for the church of God as a whole than for his own personal needs. He sends one of his best back to his own parish community.

This brother was Paul's friend and confidant. Now Paul returns him to his people to continue his work among them.

Selfishness can be a terrible problem in the church. Possessiveness of people or things can blind us to the proper way of doing things. We cannot hold on to people or to an assignment forever.

In the days before Vatican Council II, parishes had boundaries. People, by law, had to belong to the parish where they lived. The only exception was for ethnic, or language, parishes.

Today, people can join any parish that appeals to them. As a consequence, it is not unknown for pastors to literally "poach" on neighboring parishes.

For example, in a certain town, one pastor conducted his liturgy fifteen minutes later than the neighbor to catch the "latecomers." Others had "quickie" Masses on Sunday night. Others were very lax about rules. A couple could skip the instructions for baptism. Children could show up a few weeks before communion or confirmation, and be put in with those who had attended class for two years. Marriage was quick and easy to arrange. Meanwhile, the guy next door, who kept all the rules, was the "bad guy." I wonder which one Jesus will favor.

Give and gifts will be given to you. . . . —Luke 6:38

Heaven and hell are separated by our ego. If we abandon our ego, we enter the Kingdom of God.
—Willigis Jäger

Every apostolic action involves a first moment of detachment from all that is not Him. —Gustav Thils

128.

I commend to you Phoebe our sister, who is [also] a minister of the church at Cenchreae, that you may receive her in the Lord in a manner worthy of the holy ones, and help her in whatever she may need from you, for she has been a benefactor to many and to me as well.

Greet Prisca and Aquila, my co-workers in Christ Jesus, who risked their necks for my life, to whom not only I am grateful but also all the churches of the Gentiles. . . .
—Romans 16:1–4

My brother,

Paul teaches us a great deal about love and care for the female servants of God. Too often priests are chauvinistic. That is, they subconsciously feel superior to women. They often use women for their own purposes. And in many cases, they have no sensitivity for the female person. They simply take women for granted.

Paul knew well all that he owed to the women in his life. He treated them properly—as true Christians.

There is a real problem here. This is not, no matter how the media or Madison Avenue portrays it, a unisex world.

Once, in the seminary, I made the statement, "Women are different from men." The entire class, seventy-two guys (second and third year theology students) broke up in laughter.

But if a priest today is not sensitive to the female population that surrounds him, that priest is in for many stormy days.

O woman, great is your faith! —Matthew 15:28

And so I desire that all of you, together with me, should find in Mary, the Mother of Christ, the priesthood which we have all received from Christ. You must nourish human hearts with Christ. Who can make you more aware of what you are doing than she who nourished Him? —Pope John Paul II

Love is the abridgement of all theology.
—St. Francis de Sales

In their relationships with women, priests take as their model the nobility and naturalness of Jesus.
—Hans Urs Von Balthassar

PAUL: A MAN FLAWED LIKE OURSELVES

For to me life is Christ, and death is gain. —Philippians 1:21

My brother,

Again and again, remember Paul's words, "yet I live, no longer I, but Christ lives in me" (Gal 2:20). Life, for Paul, is Jesus Christ. Therefore, while he was still in the flesh, and while he was still burdened by troubles and duties, he endured them all for the sake of Christ.

Dying held no fear for Paul. It would be a release, a joy, that he anticipated. But until then, every day was spent in Christ. Does our morning offering of ourselves still consecrate our day?

Father Baker was the spiritual director at the seminary. He told us of a time in 1929 when he had to go to the bedside of a boy with a terminal disease. He told the boy that he wouldn't get better.

"Are you afraid?" asked Father Baker.

"Nah," said the boy, "I ain't done nothin'."

Would that we could say that on our deathbed.

> And I have given them the glory you gave me, so that they may be one, as we are one, I in them and you in me. . . . —John 17:22–23

> Detachment liberates the wings of our hearts, so that we can rise to the grateful enjoyment of life in all its fullness. —David Steindl-Rast

> We should always be hearing, as with bodily ears, the gurgling well-spring of our origin in God.
> —Hans Urs Von Balthassar

If we want to become spiritual stones suitable for
building up the spiritual edifice of the church, we must
accept our fate of being cut and carved. In order to be
suitable for the house, we must let ourselves be bent
into shape for the places where we are needed.
—Cardinal Ratzinger

When I flee from prayer, it's not that I want to flee from
You, but from myself and my own superficiality.
—Karl Rahner, S.J.

130.

*Paul, a slave of Christ Jesus, called to be an apostle and set
apart for the gospel of God, . . .* —Romans 1:1

My brother,
    "Set apart," in the Hebrew tongue, is *Qadosh*. It is translated
as "Holy."
    You have been set apart—sanctified for your role. You are
separated from family, home, and even some friends, because
of what you are. You have been dedicated to one task—to make
Christ known and loved.
    All else in your life is secondary and extraneous. As a person
of the world, you may be a non-entity. But as the "Holy One"
of Christ, you are everything.
    When Angelo Roncalli became the patriarch of Venice, he
had a terrible time. In the very poor Italy, when a priest became
a pastor, it was not unusual for his family to move in with him.
The cardinal wrote, "I must live apart from them [his own fam-
ily] as an example to those good Venetian clergy who . . . have
with them too many members of their families who are a con-
siderable encumbrance to their pastoral ministry in life, in
death, and after death."

As the deer longs for streams of water,
   so my soul longs for you, O God. —Psalms 42:2

Look after my interests, and I will take care of thine.
—Jesus to St. Teresa

The priestly character is ontological. It seeks to
surrender to God, not only deeds, but the very source
from which springs the doing of deeds, the human
itself, all its capacities and possibilities.
—Jean Galot, S.J.

Excessive attachment to one's own family which, when
they are felt beyond the limits of charity, becomes an
embarrassment and a hindrance. The law of the
apostolate and the priesthood is above the law of flesh
and blood. . . . My closest relations, brothers, sisters,
nephews, and nieces, are exemplary Christians but it
would never do for me to get mixed up in their affairs
and concerns so as to be diverted from my duties.
—Pope John XXIII

131.

For through the law I died to the law, that I might live for
God. I have been crucified with Christ; yet I live, no longer I,
but Christ lives in me; insofar as I now live in the flesh, I live
by faith in the Son of God who has loved me and given
himself up for me. —Galatians 2:19–20

My brother,
   These statements are not just words or clichés. Saint Paul is
not using metaphors. He is not using analogy. Paul is pointing
to an ontological reality.
   The indwelling of the Trinity is not a concept. The presence
of the Holy Spirit in our soul is not imaginary. And for the
preacher of Christ, his intense spiritual essence in our inner
mansion is not a dream. It is a vital active force always present,

yet often intangible in our core being. You belong to Christ more than you can possibly realize.

> Through these, he has bestowed on us the precious and very great promises, so that through them you may come to share in the divine nature, after escaping from the corruption that is in the world because of evil desire. —2 Peter 1:4

> It is difficult to behave with supernatural naturalness— of which the Lord gave us a perfect example—when there is artificiality. —Frederico Suarez

> Even if Christ should be born thousands of times in Bethlehem, unless He be born in you, you would be eternally lost. —Angelus Silesius

> We derive our identity ultimately from the love of the Father, we turn our gaze to the Son, sent by the Father as High Priest and Good Shepherd. Through the power of the Holy Spirit, we are united sacramentally to him in the ministerial priesthood. Our priestly life and activity continue the life and activity of Christ himself. Here lies our identity, our true dignity, the sense of our joy, the very basis of our life. —Pastores Dabo Vobis

> By virtue of sacramental ordination, the priest acquires an ontological identification with Christ which objectively imprints Christ's image on his soul, irrespective of his personal moral qualities.
> —Thomas J. McGovern

132.

> ... *such is my gospel, for which I am suffering, even to the point of chains, like a criminal. But the word of God is not chained. Therefore, I bear with everything for the sake of those who are chosen, so that they too may obtain the salvation that is in Christ Jesus, together with eternal glory.*
> —2 Timothy 2:8-10

My brother,

We have heard Paul speak often of joy in suffering. Here he reveals more clearly some of his ordeal.

Criminals in chains were abused in Paul's time, even by strangers, for there was little mercy and no respect shown by most people. Humiliation and suffering and derision are difficult to accept.

In the eyes of good people, criminals were as good as dead for they were on their way to a cruel fate.

Yet, Paul accepted everything with a good spirit for the suffering was for a purpose—the salvation of souls.

If we see current events with the eyes of faith, we can see God's plan for the world as it evolves.

There is no doubt that the collective suffering of so many Catholic priests, religious, and lay people will produce a future harvest of Christian souls for the honor and glory of God.

There should be a certain pride in being priests in this day and age. They will speak of our time in future generations as an age of heroes for Christ. We are writing another page in "Salvation History." Who knows, they may even say of us, "There were giants on the earth in those days."

> The Son of Man is to be handed over to men and they will kill him. ... —Mark 9:31

The war waged for more than eighteen hundred years
against the Catholic priest is one of the most surprising
phenomena in the history of the human race.
—Jacques Millet, S.J.

It is not then man, but Jesus Christ, who is persecuted
in the priest. —Jacques Millet, S.J.

133.

*Every day I face death; I swear it by the pride in you
[brothers] that I have in Christ Jesus our Lord.*
—1 Corinthians 15:31

My brother,

There are priests who literally face death every day. The
twentieth century was as bloody—perhaps more bloody—than
any century in history.

Great evil movements regard Christ and his church as a mortal enemy. Communism, fascism, Islamic fundamentalism, and
other movements such as the B.J.P. party in India caused terrible persecutions. So many brave priests, religious, and lay people were consumed by the holocaust for the sake of Christ.

We wonder if we could ever have their courage. Would we
yield under torture, or threats, or even before imminent
execution?

The answer is that we need not worry. Jesus said, "But
when he comes, the Spirit of truth, he will guide you to all
truth" (Jn 16:13). Jesus warned that his disciples would be put
to death. Often those who persecute you will claim that they
are serving God. ". . . in fact, the hour is coming when everyone who kills you will think he is offering worship to God"
(Jn 16:2).

Do not worry about tomorrow or doubt your courage. When
and if the time comes for a trial, you will be ready.

Padre Pro is a good model for us. He, a Jesuit, was not a rev-
olutionary figure. He was, by nature, a timid figure. Yet, he was
a priest. He lived with a full knowledge of the danger that

threatened him from an anti-Catholic communist regime that governed Mexico.

When he was finally captured and sentenced, he could stand before a firing squad and almost joyfully shout, "Viva, Christo Rey!" If put in the same position, so could you. Trust Jesus! What Padre Pro was—you are now.

> But whoever does the will of God remains forever.
> —1 John 2:17

> If love is present, it conquers all. —Jacques Millet, S.J.

> The priest is entrusted with a considerable responsibility for his task is to bring to fruition God's plan for mankind with all of his personal resourcefulness and with the resolve to be unconditionally faithful. —Jean Galot, S.J.

134.

What then is my recompense? That, when I preach, I offer the gospel free of charge so as not to make full use of my right in the gospel. —1 Corinthians 9:18

My brother,

The gospel is our treasure. We have been given it to share. Our reward is in our labor.

One of the most common attitudes among priests is this. Everyone knows about Jesus. His name and teaching are common throughout the world. The ethical teaching of Christ permeates society, even if it lies there unrecognized in the secular or non-Christian world.

But the word is not like a bath of water that covers the body, or like the air that we breathe. It is more like an incendiary fuel.

When the soul hears the word—and fully accepts it—it literally explodes in the heart. It consumes the mind and the emotions with love.

We who preach the word are the instruments of God. We provide the word. But it is the Spirit that ignites the flame of love.

> My brothers, if anyone among you should stray from the truth and someone bring him back, he should know that whoever brings back a sinner from the error of his way will save his soul from death and will cover a multitude of sins. —James 5:19

> The priest cannot impart the truth and the life of Christ, nor live by his pastoral love, without a profound commitment to the way of the cross. —Jean Galot, S.J.

> For the preacher, two things are necessary, namely that his words should be rich in ghostly wisdom, and that his life should be conspicuous for the luster of its piety. —St. Peter Damien

> The fire of God's love invites and challenges us insistently into the deep glow of peace and the radiant energy of salvation in Christ Jesus.
> —George A. Aschenbrenner, S.J.

135.

For you know how one must imitate us. For we did not act in a disorderly way among you, nor did we eat food received free from anyone. On the contrary, in toil and drudgery, night and day we worked, so as not to burden any of you. Not that we do not have the right. Rather, we wanted to present ourselves as a model for you, so that you might imitate us.
—2 Thessalonians 3:7–9

My brother,

Paul is here, in this passage, touching on a very sore point.

Priests by their vocation are respected. We are set apart for the service of the faithful. They in turn take care of our temporal needs.

How easy it is to rest in the arms of complacency. How easy to dine on good food, to sleep in a fine rectory and to have all the comforts of life.

Paul worked with his hands. Paul asked for very little. Paul expended himself in his ministry. He "imposed himself" on no one.

Lazy, selfish clerics have always plagued the church of Christ. They always will. But you, my brother, follow Paul! It will insure your salvation.

It was a shock some years back when diocesan priests had the option of choosing their own assignments. They, at one point, literally wrote down their expectations. Of course, they also had to be acceptable to the pastor of the assignment that they desired.

The requirements sought after, in many cases, were nothing short of scandalous. One fellow said that he did "liturgy—nothing else"—no phone calls, no hospital visits, no organizations, no bingo. "I do liturgy," he said, "I want absolute control of music, decorations, altar boys, lectors and Eucharistic ministers. I do liturgy and nothing else." This guy belonged on Broadway, not in the church.

Others were not ashamed to delineate money, vacations, the size of the quarters and the number of rooms, the quality of the food, and even a parish allowance to enable them to get a degree. Brothers, something was amiss in their formation.

Do not work for food that perishes but for the food that endures for eternal life. . . . —John 6:27

To become a true disciple of Christ means accepting a spirituality of the cross and renouncing a spirituality of Glory. —Ruth Burrows

The accusation of hypocrisy which is sometimes leveled at priests arises from our levity, superficiality, and lack of spiritual life. This is clearly manifest in some who are careless and too attached to the things of this world.
—Frederico Suarez

136.

Are we beginning to commend ourselves again? Or do we need, as some do, letters of recommendation to you or from you? You are our letter, written on our hearts, known and read by all, shown to be a letter of Christ administered by us, written not in ink but by the Spirit of the living God, not on tablets of stone but on tablets that are hearts of flesh.
—2 Corinthians 3:1–3

My brother,

You are a letter of Christ. Wherever you go, your very presence carries the message—Christ lives.

Do you ever realize how much you are being observed by believers and nonbelievers alike? They see in you the church, on the street, at public meetings, even when you are off recreating. You cannot hide.

Therefore, if your demeanor is pleasant, cheerful, and holy, you are reflecting the face of God. But, my friend, actions that are crude, base, and ignominious literally do damage to the church that is difficult to repair.

A newly ordained priest went on vacation with his mother to New England. He was dressed in casual clothing. One day, they decided to take a boat ride to Martha's Vineyard. The two of them were sitting there, amidst a large crowd, on the excursion boat. Suddenly a voice called out from the front of the boat, "Bless me, Father." The whole crowd laughed and looked at the priest. The man who had recognized him enjoyed the priest's embarrassment. The priest was happy that his companion was his mother.

You are God's man! You cannot escape it.

> Above all, let your love for one another be intense, because love covers a multitude of sins. —1 Peter 4:8

> You are the light of the world. (Matthew 5:14) The priesthood is the power plant from which the world receives the light of faith, of truth, of justice, of love.
> —Aloysius Biskupek, S.V.D.

> The priest speaks to men in the name of God, and to God in the name of men. —Eugene Boylan, O.C.R.

> Modern man listens more willingly to witnesses than to teachers and if he does listen to teachers, it is because they are witnesses. —Pope John Paul II

137.

My children, for whom I am again in labor until Christ be formed in you! —Galatians 4:19

My brother,

The coming of the Messiah was described by the Jews as the "birth pangs of the Messiah."

There is no doubt that worry, anxiety, pain, frustration, and even sorrow can enter into the very bones of a priest. His care and constant concern for the people entrusted to him can take its toll. Ennui and despair can invade our lives.

Take your day off! Take your vacation! Go on retreat! Go to confession! Get away regularly!

All of the above will keep the troubles away from your inner being. You need a perspective such as Paul had. After all, he was always climbing into another ship to find another adventure. We all need change.

There was a pastor whose boast was this: "I haven't had a day off in twenty years."

What he never realized was that his presence hung like a black cloud over the property. He was on everyone, over everyone, and around everyone. Like God, the man was omnipresent.

Finally, he became ill and had to go to the hospital. The priests drove him there, cheerfully. When the doctors ordered him to a rest home for a month, the whole staff was ecstatic. When he finally arrived home, he was amazed to see how well the parish had done without him.

On a good day enjoy good things, and on an evil day consider: Both the one and the other God has made, so that man cannot find fault with him in anything.
—Ecclesiastes 7:14

Man is free, certainly, but it is important that he should also feel free when he does what he wants because he wants to do it. —Frederico Suarez

No one can live without some minimum of happiness and pleasure. —Frederico Suarez

138.

From now on, let no one make troubles for me; for I bear the marks of Jesus on my body. —Galatians 6:17

My brother,

I never met a stigmatic, one who is a saint like Padre Pio. They are very rare. Their purpose is to inject a consciousness of the Lord and the supernatural into an unbelieving world.

But I have met many priests who bear the marks of Christ on their bodies. I have seen priests whose faces are lined with years of caring for people. I have seen priests whose bodies are bent with years of hard labor in the vineyard of the Lord. I have seen the ravaged bodies of priests who poured out their lives in service.

Yes, I can look in the eyes of older men and see there a love that is gentle and kind, that is the product of years of self-denial in the service of others.

Yes, friend, many, many of our brothers bear the marks of Christ in their body. They wear the stigmata of the Lord.

One of the great joyful places of our priestly world can be the retirement home. There, it is almost as if the days of the seminary have been recreated. The bodies may be aged. The steps may be slower. But the humor, the personalities, the characters, and the memories of the past are all alive. When you are with them, it is as if time had melted away.

Have you visited any of the older priests lately? Go! You will have a wonderful time.

I will pay my vows to the Lord
in the presence of all his people. —Psalms 116:14

Morning by morning, at the altar, you fill your bosom with fire. —Jacques Millet, S.J.

Priests will gain sanctity in a manner proper to them if they exercise their office sincerely and tirelessly—in the spirit of Christ.
—Decree on the Ministry and Life of Priests

139.

About this person I will boast, but about myself I will not boast, except about my weaknesses . . . because of the abundance of the revelations. Therefore, that I might not become too elated, a thorn in the flesh was given to me, an angel of Satan, to beat me, to keep me from being too elated. Three times I begged the Lord about this, that it might leave me, but he said to me, "My grace is sufficient for you, for power is made perfect in weakness." I will rather boast most gladly of my weaknesses, in order that the power of Christ may dwell with me. Therefore, I am content with weaknesses, insults, hardships, persecutions, and constraints, for the sake of Christ; for when I am weak, then I am strong.
—2 Corinthians 12:5, 7–10

My brother,

There is a mystery about this "thorn in the flesh," this "angel of Satan," that beat Paul and kept him from getting proud. What was the thorn? It could have been physical—perhaps sensual temptation. It could have been psychological—periods of depression, or fear, or doubt.

Brother, you, like Paul, carry in your own being a "thorn in the flesh." And, like Paul, it is probably known only to you and your confessor or spiritual director. No man is perfect. Saint

John reminds us that the man who claims that he has no sin lies. The fact is that a man who thinks he is sinless is blind to his faults.

But all that is irrelevant. Brother, your weakness, your failing, your fault is your burden and your cross. God says to you as he said to Paul, my power reaches perfection in weakness. Your weakness, my friend, is God's opportunity. All he asks is that you persevere. Don't give up! Don't give up! There is a strength in you and with you that you neither know nor understand. It is the Creator filling your emptiness with his presence.

One of the problems with the spiritual life of the priesthood was the constant presentation of ideals that most of us could never follow. We were supposed to imitate the saints. In the days before Vatican Council II, for example, the Cure of Ars was practically presented as our role model. The Cure of Ars ate one potato a week. He was a super-ascetic.

In our seminary, one man fasted so much that his fingernails fell off. It cost $40 a week in vitamins and medicines just to bring him back to health. The spiritual director said of him, "Oh my, he's just a little nervous." Two years after ordination, he disappeared. Then he reappeared in a mental hospital.

Thank the Lord for modern psychology—and for saints of today who are believable and can be imitated.

All things are possible for God. —Mark 10:27

The opposition of the "dark tyrant" within us is so powerful that this [inner] self must slowly be broken up to the last grain, like a rock under continual attack from the waves. It must crumble away, rot, burn up until it is finally open. —Hans Urs Van Balthassar

We stumble and we fall constantly, even when we are most enlightened. But when we are in true spiritual darkness we do not even know that we have fallen. —Thomas Merton

140.

When you come, bring the cloak I left with Carpus in Troas, the papyrus rolls, and especially the parchments.
—2 Timothy 4:13

My brother,

This always causes some amusement, because here we find the great apostle, the mighty preacher, the founder of churches seemingly brought to earth in a small mundane matter. When you come, would you bring me my coat? And my books?

This is a good reminder to us that all great men have much in common with the rest of men. They have bodily needs. They put their shoes on each day in the same way that we do. They have to eat and bathe and take care of their bodies like all ordinary mortals.

Also, great people, no matter how great they are, need people. No man is an island. There are very, very few true hermits.

The lesson for us is this. Since we are all human, all part of the same human family, then we are all in some way interdependent. The church is the Mystical Body People need people.

There are two extremes. Some priests act as if they are superior beings—just because they are priests. That is a fatal flaw in the man of God. They expect that others will defer to them.

However, some of us try to do everything ourselves. This flaw can be destructive because we actually deprive others. We do not allow them full freedom of the children of God. We give them little, perhaps no, chance to participate in building up the house of God, to share in the work of God.

Brother, do not keep those at arm's length who want to share the apostolate. Jesus never did. He welcomed all followers. We need all the help we can get. So did Saint Paul.

Greet one another with a loving kiss. —1 Peter 5:14

The priest is the man who serves God. The minister is a servant. —Jean Galot, S.J.

The fact of ordination does not provide technical competence, pedagogical talents, or scientific erudition.
—Gustav Thils

In Christianity, there should be no second-class Christians.
—Thomas Vernon Moore, M.D., Carthusian

141.

Be imitators of me, as I am of Christ. —1 Corinthians 11:1

Join with others in being imitators of me, brothers, and observe those who thus conduct themselves according to the model you have in us. —Philippians 3:17

My brother,

This, of all Paul's admonitions, is a true "heart stopper." Who can perform the role perfectly of a truly apostolic man?

Imitation is the greatest form of flattery. All of us can imitate the Lord in some things. It is obvious that no one—except perhaps a Francis of Assisi—can become a walking image of the Savior.

So, in this, brothers, it is well for us to look not at Jesus, but at Paul. Paul tried to imitate Jesus, but any study of Paul's life and words reveal that Paul was a flawed character. He was impatient, abrupt, judgmental, at times, even threatening. He took offense poorly. This Paul, who tells us to imitate him, is not speaking about achieved perfection of life.

He is speaking of our own intention. He is speaking of our desire and our resolve to go through life as Jesus did. *Pertransivit benefaciendo*—He passed through doing good.

So, in your heart, try to be another Paul, and leave the rest to the Lord. He will shape and form you through a lifetime of experiences. Trust in God! He is the potter. We are the clay.

Any priest who has the care of property needs the patience of a saint. And, if the priest happens to be a "Type A" personality, he will find himself driven at times to distraction. In some cases, the man might need a straightjacket.

In a parish church, school, rectory, convent, or church structure, what is everybody's business is nobody's business. Things are broken. The toilets are stopped up. Windows are left open in the wintertime. Lights are left burning day and night. Doors are left unlocked. Things disappear. When the person in charge asks, "Who did this?" no one knows. No one ever admits to anything. The only conclusion is that ghosts or gremlins live on the property. It is no wonder if the man in charge might need some form of tranquilizer.

Children, let us love not in word or speech but in deed and truth. —1 John 3:18

Do not have Jesus Christ on your lips and the world in your hearts. —St. Ignatius of Antioch

Priests will find great help in the possession of those virtues which are deservedly esteemed in human affairs—such as goodness of heart, sincerity, strength, constancy of character, zealous pursuit of justice, civility, and those other traits which the apostle Paul recommends. —Jean Galot, S.J.

PART TWO

Guiding the
Community of God

ONE IN THE SPIRIT, ONE IN THE LORD:
WE ALL NEED HELP

142.

. . . in the household of God, which is the church of the living God, the pillar and foundation of truth. —1 Timothy 3:15

My brother,

In the seminary, we studied two ways to discover the truth of God's church. One way was the *via descendens*, wherein we studied the great foundations of the church and then compared it with the church today. We would find that the church of the apostles and our own community are basically the same.

The other is the *via ascendens*. We studied our church in all of its glory, and with all of its faults, and then traveled back with the church over the centuries. We find that the church is a "moral miracle." There is nothing like it on the face of God's earth.

All sorts of creeds, groups, and "isms" have come and gone. Yet, Christ and his apostles, disciples, and community have propagated themselves over the years. This church has withstood every form of fault, corruption, and heresy. She remains the unspotted, unwrinkled beautiful bride of the Lamb.

It is so easy to forget our history. It is so easy to lose sight of Christ's Mystical Body Yet, turn on the television. If you wait, inevitably, Rome will appear. And, while many hate the church, they all grant her just one great accomplishment. She survives. She grows. She is unquestionably special—even to those who deny her.

> I also saw the holy city, a new Jerusalem, coming down out of heaven from God, prepared as a bride adorned for her husband. —Revelation 21:2

All things are veils, behind which is hidden a mystery.
—Blaise Pascal

In the Eucharist, the faithful are nourished and grow
strong at the same table, and in a Divine ineffable way
are brought into union with each other and with the
Divine Head of the whole body. —Mystici Corporis

For priests are brothers among brothers with all those
who have been reborn at the baptismal font. They are
all members of the one and same Body of Christ, whose
upbuilding is entrusted to all.
—Decree on the Ministry and Life of Priests

143.

*And he gave some as apostles, others as prophets, others as
evangelists, others as pastors and teachers, to equip the holy
ones for the work of ministry, for building up the body of
Christ. . . .* —Ephesians 4:11, 12

My brother,
    In the world of construction, every tool has a specific pur-
pose. Every machine is composed of various parts that are
essential.
    Many human beings are "wannabes." They want to be some-
thing that they are not.
    Many priests, especially when they are young, have the
same problem. It is not as difficult now as it once was. The
church gives us much more freedom to fit our natural apti-
tudes into the ministry that suits us best.
    Yet, face it, we are what we are. Much of what we desire is
just that, vain desire. "Lord, what would thou have me do?"
must be our final and most important prayer.
    Apostles are daring men of action. Prophets must be willing
to suffer for speaking words that many do not want to hear.
Pastors must lead and guide all of the flock, not just the most
compliant. Evangelists must stand in the marketplace where

they are just one voice in a cacophony of sound. Teachers will often find tedium in teaching the same lessons over and over.

Brother, count your blessings. After thinking of many apostolates, most of us discover that we are where we should be— where God wants us—and where we will be most happy.

> I glorified you on earth by accomplishing the work that you gave me to do. —John 17:4

> There is nothing which provides better instruction for others unto piety and worship of God than the life and example of those who have dedicated themselves to the divine ministry. —The Council of Trent

> Christian obedience, and thus diocesan priestly obedience, is always chiefly motivated and determined by the experience of God's love. —George A. Aschenbrenner, S.J.

> The voluntary acceptance of the divine call to the priesthood was, without a doubt, an act of love which makes each of us a lover. —Pope John Paul II

144.

> *. . . and all of them were baptized into Moses in the cloud and in the sea. All ate the same spiritual food, and all drank the same spiritual drink, for they drank from a spiritual rock that followed them, and the rock was the Christ.*
> —1 Corinthians 10:2–4

My brother,

This mystical reference symbolizes our life as priests.

We operate in the present. Yet, our daily life centers on a mystery that recreates the past sacrifice of Christ in an invisible manner. We see bread and wine. We sense the transformation that enables us to commune with the living Lord.

In the same way, our roots go deep into the mists of time. In God, there is no before, no after, no change of being. All is timeless.

So, as we now make Christ present again in an invisible way, so Christ was present in some mysterious way before the "Word" became flesh.

The Israelites touched and were touched by the presence of the Creator. All that they did was somehow proleptic, it reached forward into time. The manna, while not yet Eucharist, was the foreshadowing of that which was to come. That strange rock poured forth water that prefigured the life-giving grace which would pour forth from the crucified and risen one.

Brother, your very life is mystery. One day, you will understand it. Now, just try to "experience" rather than understand the sanctity of who and what you are.

. . . do this in memory of me. —Luke 22:19

To the priest, the Eucharist is everything. It is his all.
—Jacques Millet, S.J.

The Eucharist shows itself to be the source and apex of the whole work of preaching the gospel.
—Decree on the Ministry and Life of Priests

The Eucharist could not exist without us; but without the Eucharist, we do not exist, we are reduced to lifeless shadows. —Pope John Paul II

145.

. . . even as Christ loved the church and handed himself over for her to sanctify her, cleansing her by the bath of water with the word, that he might present to himself the church in splendor, without spot or wrinkle or any such thing, that she might be holy and without blemish. —Ephesians 5:25–27

My brother,

This church, spiritually and ideally, is holy and immaculate without stain or wrinkle. That is because, as in the prophecy of Ezekiel, she has been washed clean and has a "new heart,"— that is, in reality, the Holy Spirit.

However, the concrete expression of this holy church on earth is often far from lovely. Her stains, her wrinkles, and her faults are apparent for all to see for they are visible in the thoughts, the intentions, and the lives of those of whom she is composed. Therefore, the visible church sadly manifests herself in ways that are not perfect. But oh, the invisible church, that mystical body of Christ which has the Holy Spirit as her soul is terribly, awfully beautiful. She transcends the sum of her parts as this church to shine upon the world as Christ's true sun—giving light to all of the nations.

> Behold, God's dwelling is with the human race. He will dwell with them and they will be his people and God himself will always be with them [as their God].
> —Revelation 21:3

> If some members of the church are spiritually ill that is no reason why we should lessen our love for the Church, but rather a reason why we should increase our devotion to her members. —Pius XII

> There is but one man—Christ—who reaches to the end of time and those that cry out are always His members. —St. Augustine

> The most private kind of tabernacle devotion is a realization of membership in the church, of responsibility to her; an apostolate of prayer in a very genuine and profound sense. —Karl Rahner, S.J.

146.

Let every person be subordinate to the higher authorities, for there is no authority except from God, and those that exist have been established by God. Therefore, whoever resists authority opposes what God has appointed, and those who oppose it will bring judgment upon themselves.
—Romans 13:1, 2

My brother,

Herein lies a test. Authority in an earthly, civil sense can be good or bad. Sometimes, by their deeds and their ideas, some rulers forfeit their right to exercise authority. At times, civil disobedience may not only be an option, but a necessity. So it was for Christian pastors under Hitler.

However, in the church, we must accept divine providence as a regular norm. Those who wield power in the church may, at times, be wrong in their judgments in certain areas. Sometimes, it seems as if the wrong people are in charge. In some cases, good Catholic people may feel that their leaders live in a surrealistic world completely out of touch with reality.

But bear with it, friend, bear with it. The church works in time, but from the aspect of eternity. All things pass. And even though we cannot see it now, the hand of God is there. Even the most stupid, meaningless laws and events can have a purpose. Trust in the Lord.

In our own day, we have seen the mighty brought low. The scandal of pedophilia has rocked the church. Some of the most powerful men in the hierarchy have been accused, attacked, and vilified. Some have been driven from office.

Some in the hierarchy were "cruelly kind." They tried to protect unworthy priests. They tried to shield the church from shame. It all ended by taking a terrible toll on the church, the priests, and the people. Yes, some bishops were paralyzed by the very fear of scandal. Some were misled by psychologists. Some, evidently, were given bad advice by those around them. Some were just plain stupid.

Corruptio optimi, pessimus. The fall from the heights is a terrible thing to watch.

These bishops are priests and brothers. We need to pray for them. And then turn our eyes to those good men who still hold the title of *"episcopus"*—overseer.

They need the help, prayers, and comfort of the presbyterate. Together, we will get through this. The church of the twenty-first century is being reborn—holy, immaculate, and undefiled.

> Yours, O LORD, are grandeur and power,
>   majesty, splendor, and glory.
> For all in heaven and on earth is yours. . . .
> —1 Chronicles 29:11

> The priest cannot measure supernatural work by purely human yardsticks or by the standards of this world.
> —Frederico Suarez

> The superior may not be as perfect as his office would make us expect, yet he does not, on account of his weakness, cease being a superior.
> —Aloysius Biskupek, S.V.D.

147.

Obey your leaders and defer to them, for they keep watch over you and will have to give an account, that they may fulfill their task with joy and not with sorrow, for that would be of no advantage to you. —Hebrews 13:17

My brother,

Aren't you happy, in a way, that you only have limited responsibility for the souls of other men? If you are a pastor, or a bishop, you will render an account of your stewardship.

However, you can only act on your best judgment, and often with counsel from others. But you must do what you must do. Once you have examined your conscience, once you have weighed an issue, and you have obtained the best advice possible, then, my friend, you must act.

The key, however, is that you must act with a serene conscience. Fulfill your task with joy, and the Lord will give you peace.

For others of us who have responsibility for souls in other ways than as superiors, the same counsel holds true. Think, pray, and get counsel. Then act with a pure heart, joyfully. The Holy Spirit is with you.

> Father, if you are willing, take this cup away from me; still, not my will but yours be done. —Luke 22:42

> Justice is never fully ministered on earth and often the priest is unjustly judged by men.
> —Aloysius Biskupek, S.V.D.

> The art of arts is the direction of souls.
> —Jacques Millet, S.J.

> The office of pastor is not confined to the care of the faithful as individuals, but is also properly extended to the formation of a genuine Christian community.
> —Decree on the Ministry and Life of Priests

> The Bishops are more exposed to the temptation of meddling immoderately in matters that are not their concern. —Pope John XXIII

GOD'S PURE GIFT: HIMSELF AS PURE CHARITY

148.

For I take delight in the law of God, in my inner self, but I see in my members another principle at war with the law of my mind, taking me captive to the law of sin that dwells in my members. Miserable one that I am! Who will deliver me from this mortal body? Thanks be to God through Jesus Christ our Lord. Therefore, I myself, with my mind, serve the law of God but, with my flesh, the law of sin.
—Romans 7:22–25

My brother,

These words are those of a genius. No one has ever described the human condition better than Paul.

The Jews had an expression for this state—*yetzer ha ra, yetzer ha tov.* "*Yetzer ha ra*" meant a pull to evil, "*yetzer ha tov*" meant a pull to the good.

Paul describes this human state in terms of spirit versus flesh. The spirit draws us to all that is good, pure, holy, and otherworldly.

The flesh, on the other hand, imprisons the soul and traps it in a myriad of desires, yearnings, cravings, and hungers.

Ascetics went to war with their bodies. But to be truthful, the way of unbridled asceticism can lead to weakness, neurasthenia, and ultimately to a worse state than if we had acted more normally. It is a dangerous, and sometimes slippery slope.

No, my friend, our war against the flesh must not be violent. It must be fought day by day in little things. If we follow some sort of priestly rule in our lives, then that rule will carry us. A gentle effort to bring order into our lives is far better than frantic strivings.

With perseverance, we shall overcome our weaknesses. Maybe not today. Maybe not tomorrow. But surely one day, the spirit will soar like the eagle. The old temptations, no matter of what sort they be, will lessen and we will be free—gloriously free.

> . . . sin is a demon lurking at the door. —Genesis 4:7

> The consciousness of each of us is evolution looking at itself and reflecting. —Pierre Teilhard de Chardin, S.J.

> Through the fountain-fullness of the Word came the embrace of God's love, which nourishes us into life, is our help in our perils, and, as a most profound and gentle love, opens us up for repentance.
> —Hildegarde of Bingen

> What we do to sanctify ourselves, sanctifies the world.
> —Bishop Fulton J. Sheen

149.

Make no mistake: God is not mocked, for a person will reap only what he sows, because the one who sows for his flesh will reap corruption from the flesh, but the one who sows for the spirit will reap eternal life from the spirit.
—Galatians 6:7, 8

My brother,

Paul continues his spirit versus flesh theme.

Original sin is a problem. Everyone suffers from the human condition. It is a part of life's condition.

But Paul is speaking above, not of the struggle, win or lose, but of the man who deceives himself, his neighbor, and believes he is deceiving God himself.

Put your treasure where your heart is. If you are a spiritual man, then the things of the flesh should not be your goal. What a horror it can be to see a priest engaged in business. How sad to know a priest who wants to live his life in ease, in wealth, in sensuality, and then pretends to be righteous to other men.

What a scandal erupted when one priest died, and it was discovered that he was the owner of a huge number of apartments in the city. It was even more of a scandal when it was discovered that he was a slumlord.

What are your priorities, my friend? When you get up each day, what is it that you look forward to? What are your goals? Answer honestly and you will discover your true value system. Is it God—or something earthly? Only you can know.

No servant can serve two masters. He will either hate one and love the other, or be devoted to one and despise the other. You cannot serve God and mammon. —Luke 16:13

He who is willingly poor is free and without the cares of this world's goods. —John Ruysbroek

There are men dedicated to God whose lives are devoured by activities and strangled with attachments. Interior solitude is impossible for them. —Thomas Merton

Burnout is not the result of the amount of work or ministry that one does, rather, it is caused by having unrealistic expectations of oneself. —Brother Loughlan Sofield, S.T.

150.

The sting of death is sin. . . . —1 Corinthians 15:56

For the wages of sin is death, but the gift of God is eternal life in Christ Jesus our Lord. —Romans 6:23

My brother,

You know sin. It is the ultimate reason for our need of redemption. It is the proximate reason for our daily confrontation with the social problems of our age.

Sin fills prisons. Sin destroys families. Sin ruins lives and causes immeasurable pain to our parishioners.

Sin affects us personally. It can cripple our ministry and destroy our power to manifest Christ to the world.

Yet, sin is in reality a nothing. According to Saint Thomas, it is a lack of due rectitude in our actions. It is a turning away from God—from justice.

Ultimately, sin, like a disease, can hollow out the soul and leave but a shell of apparent righteousness. Like a fatal disease, it can lead to a spiritual, and even a physical, death.

My brother, you are in a daily war with sin, externally in others and internally in your own life.

Yet sin can never conquer. Our Lord has destroyed sin and death together on the cross. You will be holy. I repeat, you will be holy. And, ultimately, when you take your last earthly breath, death itself will disappear in life. Christ has conquered. Glory will fill you.

> How can I repay the LORD
> for all the good done for me? —Psalms 116:12

> A recollected and interior life is absolutely necessary for the priest. —Jacques Millet, S.J.

> Human virtues are all those moral habits which any man should have if he isn't a Christian, and which a Christian raises to the supernatural level through grace.
> —Del Portillo

> The Christian life to be aimed at cannot be reduced to a mediocre commitment to "goodness" as society defines it. It must be a true quest for holiness.
> —Thomas J. McGovern

151.

The concern of the flesh is death, but the concern of the spirit is life and peace. For the concern of the flesh is hostility toward God; it does not submit to the law of God, nor can it; and those who are in the flesh cannot please God. But you are not in the flesh; on the contrary, you are in the spirit, if only the Spirit of God dwells in you. Whoever does not have the Spirit of Christ does not belong to him. But if Christ is in you, although the body is dead because of sin, the spirit is alive because of righteousness. If the Spirit of the one who raised Jesus from the dead dwells in you, the one who raised Christ from the dead will give life to your mortal bodies also, through his Spirit that dwells in you. Consequently, brothers, we are not debtors to the flesh, to live according to the flesh. For if you live according to the flesh, you will die, but if by the spirit you put to death the deeds of the body, you will live.
—Romans 8:6–13

My brother,

We have spoken of the *"yetzer ha ra"* and the *"yetzer ha tov"* of the Jewish dispensation. The tendency spoken of by Saint Paul is exactly the same theme. He hits it again and again, because he wants us to realize the extent of this struggle within us.

We are almost schizophrenic morally. We are all, in some way, Dr. Jekyll and Mr. Hyde. There are forces at war within us. These forces cause tension.

In some people, they are not as pronounced. Life is simple. Goodness outweighs evil so utterly that some fortunate people literally radiate peace.

But there are others of us who are passionate. We are the "Type A" personality, the doer, the shaker, the mover. And in our being, deep down, good wrestles with evil.

But think of it this way. Great saints were not men of meek, spineless character. They were not, to use a colloquial expression, "macaroni without salt." No. They took big bites of life.

Enormous appetites for evil can also be found in a person with a huge appetite for life and holiness.

So, don't worry about your instincts, my friend; your greatest weakness probably contains the seeds of your greatest virtue.

> As the deer longs for streams of water,
> so my soul longs for you, O God. —Psalms 42:2

> A dreamer can never be a fighter for it is easier to take refuge in the fictitious world of the imagination.
> —Frederico Suarez

> *"Quod illi potuerunt, cur non ego?"* If they could, why not I? —St. Augustine

> Man can fully discover his true self only in a sincere giving of self. —Gaudium et Spes

> The success of Alcoholics Anonymous derives from their own insistence on the appeal to God for help.
> —Thomas Vernon Moore, M.D., Carthusian

152.

But the gift is not like the transgression. For if by that one person's transgression the many died, how much more did the grace of God and the gracious gift of the one person Jesus Christ overflow for the many. —Romans 5:15

My brother,

One man died for all men. That is true. However, that one man, Jesus, was not a lone ranger.

He gathered others to himself. He shared a ministry with them. He trained them and then empowered them.

In the old theology books, the sacraments were described as fonts of grace—fountains of living water. The imagery is, perhaps, primitive. However, it is still quite accurate.

You are not a minister who relies only on words to change hearts. You have in your hands power. You are no tinkling bell or brass cymbal. You dispense life—not just an imaginary life—but an ontological reality that touches and transforms souls.

If, my friend, you ever forget—or worse, doubt—that what you do is effective in creating God's gift in the human soul, go back to your theology. Read the Fathers. Make a retreat and contemplate your role.

There is nothing like the priesthood on the face of the earth. That is why men respect you. You are a divine life giver. That is why they happily call you "Father."

You are one with Christ—the dispenser of the grace of God for the life of all.

> As each one has received a gift, use it to serve one
> another as good stewards of God's varied grace.
> —1 Peter 4:10

> God did not call on anyone to aid Him in the work of
> creation. He wished to have others assist Him in the
> work of redemption. —Peter de Blois

> In every sacramental act he performs, the priest
> infallibly sets in motion the action of the eternal
> mediator to render to the Trinity praise—or to transmit
> life to mankind. —Gustav Thils

> Priests will attain sanctity in a manner proper to them if
> they exercise their offices sincerely and tirelessly in a
> spirit of Christ.
> —Decree on the Ministry and Life of Priests

153.

*For all of you who were baptized into Christ have clothed
yourselves with Christ. There is neither Jew nor Greek, there
is neither slave nor free person, there is not male and female;
for you are all one in Christ Jesus.* —Galatians 3:27, 28

My brother,

This world has certainly become more homogenized.
People, desperate for a better life, are pouring across the bor-
ders from the Third World into Europe and the United States.
Not since the fifth century has there been such a movement of
peoples of different ethnic origins.

So, for many of us, to see the face of the church all we need
do is to look at our congregation on any given Sunday morning. But this is only the beginning.

What a terrible strain these movements can put upon our
priests. They ask us to be "all things to all men" (1 Cor 9:22). It
is easy to say, but how many languages can they ask us to
learn? How many foreign customs can they ask us to accommodate? Life, for many of us, is exceedingly difficult.

My brother, if you find yourself in a changing parish, or a
changing community, do not be depressed or saddened. You
are seeing the future when the one, holy, catholic church will
bring the living Christ to every corner of the globe.

Some day, the people of the future will look back and call the
priests of today heroes. They will bless you.

Believe it or not, priests years ago had, in some respects, a
much easier task than today. Immigrant groups came to
America. Their priests came with them. They built national (or
language) parishes where all of the devotions and customs of
their native land could be reproduced.

Today, in some city parishes, there are two or three communities vying for space. They compete for time. Their feasts and
social activities demand attention.

Meanwhile, the priests try their best to accommodate everyone. It takes the wisdom of Solomon and the patience of Job to
work things out. Paul may say there is neither Jew nor Greek,

but he never tried to operate a city parish in the United States of America.

I have other sheep that do not belong to this fold. These also I must lead, and they will hear my voice. . . .
—John 10:16

Christ did not choose apostolic functionaries, but apostles in their whole persons. —Gustav Thils

I believe that priests by virtue of their ordination have a higher and more holy state which demands of them many works of perfection. —Frederico Suarez

154.

This is the will of God, your holiness. . . .
—1 Thessalonians 4:3

My brother,

It is certainly God's will that we grow in holiness. But growth, by its very nature, is an incremental process. The only time we can actually see organic growth in nature is by slow motion photography. We cannot see a bud blossom. It just happens.

So, my friend, if you want to see where you are, do not look at yesterday. Gaze way back over the years. See where you were then, and see where you are now.

Isn't it true that, as we gaze back, we are actually embarrassed at some of the things we said and did? Were we not foolish in some things? Did we not judge more rashly and speak more foolishly in our younger years?

Sometimes we are embarrassed by the things that we say or do by accident.

My friend John, a priest in a Paterson parish, was conducting the Saint Gerard Novena one evening. At the end of the novena each Tuesday, they blessed any woman who wanted to have a baby. John's announcement came out of his mouth in these words, "Would all blessed women who wish to be pregnant meet me in the sacristy right after Mass."

John was surprised when the entire congregation broke into laughter. He was shocked later to learn why they were laughing.

You are in process. Don't be in a hurry. God is with you. Time mellows all things—even case hardened priests.

> See how the farmer waits for the precious fruit of the earth, being patient with it until it receives the early and the late rains. You too must be patient.
> —James 5:7–8

> Where there is patience and humility, there is neither anger nor worry. —St. Francis of Assisi

> All God wishes is to be the sole object and the only enchantment of the present moment.
> —Jean Pierre de Caussade

> They [the faithful] honor the priest, not because he is educated, learned, or a competent social worker, but because he alone is deputed to offer their sacrifice.
> —Raymond A. Tartre, S.S.S.

> In the contemporary culture of autonomy and independence, apology and sorrow seems weak and cowardly, often embarrassingly so.
> —George A. Aschenbrenner, S.J.

155.

Do you not know that your body is a temple of the holy Spirit within you, whom you have from God, and that you are not your own? For you have been purchased at a price. Therefore, glorify God in your body. —1 Corinthians 6:19–20

My brother,

"You are not your own." Your consecration has removed you from the secular world. The Holy Spirit dwells in a special way in that sacred space called your soul.

Now, it is obvious that there are few priests who fully realize their total consecration, the total sanctification of their very being.

Yet, the people sense it. How many are delighted when you bless their children and place your hand on their heads? How many sick or elderly feel better immediately when a priest anoints them? How many want to shake your hand and simply feel your touch?

God is glorified in your body, my friend. The fact is that we so often fail to recognize that our sacerdotal ordination has transformed our lives. We are truly vessels of grace. So, let your presence be felt. In the eyes of the people, you are as holy as any pope or bishop. In the eyes of the faithful, you carry the Lord in your person.

And now I will no longer be in the world, but they are in the world, while I am coming to you. —John 17:11

Ordinary contact with God takes place where your fellow men, your yearnings, your work, and your affections are. It is in the midst of the most material things of the earth that we most sanctify ourselves. —Msgr. Escriva de Balaguer

Go forward, ye priests of God, with your hearts filled with confidence and courage. For the Man-God goes before you. —Jacques Millet, S.J.

All through our priestly life, we have to face the challenge of availability and accessibility on countless occasions. —Thomas J. McGovern

156.

. . . and be renewed in the spirit of your minds, and put on the new self, created in God's way in righteousness and holiness of truth. —Ephesians 4:23–24

My brother,

Paul recommends a fresh spiritual way of thinking. For those of us who are, if we can put it this way, in the business of religion, that fresh new way must occur every so often. That is why the church wisely recommends a retreat every year, and vacations, and a day off every week.

Not many men live where they work. Not many are at the beck and call of the laity at almost every moment of the day. Not many people are required to pour out their lives so constantly and completely.

So, you need to stop now and then, step back, take a deep breath, and reflect on where you have been and where you are going. You need to experience the peace and quiet, the presence of God's love. In short, you need to re-create your spiritual life in Christ.

The "new man" thus produced will have the vitality and eagerness of the newly ordained priest. He will also have the benefit of experience. When these two come together—energy and wisdom—this new priest will do wonders for the Lord.

> People were coming and going in great numbers, and they had no opportunity even to eat. So they [Jesus and the apostles] went off in the boat by themselves to a deserted place. —Mark 6:31–32

Temporary solitude from all things in life, the meditation within yourself about the Divine, is food as necessary for your soul as material food is for your body. —Leo Tolstoy

The unexamined life is not worth living. —Socrates

You've got to take time, otherwise, we're running around, doing great work, but it's not connected. —Dean Hoge

Compulsive ministry often gets on people's nerves and does not witness nearly enough to God's love. —George A. Aschenbrenner, S.J.

157.

. . . so stand firm and do not submit again to the yoke of slavery. —Galatians 5:1

My brother,

Paul was addressing converts. Therefore, he was speaking of the "freedom of the sons of God." These people had been slaves to religions that were myths and dreams. They were wind and smoke. However, they held millions in captivity.

We priests never knew such a slavery to the non-existent. However, when we decided to give our lives to God, we broke with another form of slavery, the desire for earthly riches. We surrendered the possibility of having a family, of amassing wealth, and even of becoming powerful in a human political way.

Paul reminds us that we must be wary lest the things of the secular world entice us once again. The devil can hide himself under the guise of an angel.

Let us face reality. Many priests have left the priesthood after they had extended a priestly hand to a widowed woman with children. It was not lust that caused them to leave the priesthood. It was because that woman and her children became his family. It was a desire to care for someone, to belong, that led them away from the ministerial priesthood. It was all hidden under the façade of an act of charity—caring for a widow and her family.

Others found an apostolate. The apostolate seemed to have great motives and to be under the influence of the Spirit. But deep down, there was often a rebellious spirit that desired freedom, a cause to promote and a new way to live independently of the structured church.

My brother, recognize who and what you are. You are another Christ. All of your people are your family. In Christ, you have all the wealth and power that you need. You are fulfilled in Christ.

> For where your treasure is, there also will your heart be.
> —Matthew 6:21

> Love is swift, sincere, pious, pleasant, generous, strong, patient, faithful, prudent, long-suffering, manly, and never seeking its own; for wheresoever a man seeketh his own, there he falleth from love. —Thomas à Kempis

> Whoever offers sacrifice should participate in the sacrifice, because the external sacrifice which is offered is the sign of the interior sacrifice.
> —St. Thomas Aquinas

> The instinct for liking pleasure and fearing pain is understandable and healthy.
> —George A. Aschenbrenner, S.J.

158.

They are justified freely [undeservedly justified] by his grace through the redemption in Christ Jesus. —Romans 3:24

My brother,

The key word is "undeservedly" justified. What did we do, what could we ever have done, to merit all that God has bestowed on us?

He it was who gave us life. He it was who gave us our abilities. He it was who called us.

Every day, we say in the office, "Open my lips, O Lord, and my mouth will proclaim your praise."

Should we not praise the Lord at all times with his praise ever in our mouths? What can I render to the Lord for all of the good he has done to me?

My brother, it would be the very height of unjustified egotism to claim anything as our own. Every breath we take is his gift. We don't even advert to our own life processes. They happen according to his design.

So, rejoice, my friend. There is never any need for sadness. You are God's creation. You rest under the shadow of his wings. You are. He is. Alleluia.

I bore you up on eagle wings. . . . —Exodus 19:4

I am the great food. Grow and partake of me; I will not be changed into you, but you will be changed into me. —St. Augustine

We always have cause for optimism, for not being depressed, if we learn not to take ourselves too seriously. —Thomas J. McCarthy

There is, in each of us, a deepest central point where evil cannot reach and where only the beauty of God's creative love exists in all its uniqueness. —George A. Aschenbrenner, S.J.

159.

Therefore, whoever thinks he is standing secure should take care not to fall. No trial has come to you but what is human. God is faithful and will not let you be tried beyond your strength; but with the trial he will also provide a way out, so that you may be able to bear it. —1 Corinthians 10:12, 13

My brother,

Perhaps you might want to consider Paul's words, "He will give you a way out of it."

In each of our priestly lives, tests will come. Projects will fail. Dreams will disappear. Hopes will shatter. People will fail us. Things will not work out.

In many cases, there will be fear, anxiety, worry, and then despair. Sometimes, we will want to throw in the towel and just quit. "Why beat your head against a wall?" "Who cares anyway?" "What is the use of trying? I always lose."

Brother, do not let the devil gain a hold upon your heart. Look at the cross. Jesus was a loser. Jesus was embarrassed by his confreres who abandoned him. Jesus ended up broke, broken, and alone.

But, there is always an Easter Sunday. God doesn't care if you tried and lost. He is more honored because you tried. And what you consider a loss, in his eyes may be your greatest triumph.

In Christ, there are no winners or losers. We are all winners.

The history of the Catholic Church in the United States is littered with the stories of men who were ahead of their time— good priests—who paid a price for following their conscience.

Consider the scripture scholars who ran afoul of the hierarchy for opening the eyes of the church to the true nature of the scriptures and paid a price. Fathers Henry Poels (1909) and Edward Siegman (1962) were dismissed from Catholic University of America, and the scripture scholars of America came under severe attack before Vatican Council II. Consider a man like Monsignor John Kiley in the Archdiocese of Newark who created the CYO program, the Archdiocesan newspaper, and who literally lived with the derelicts of humanity in the Mount Carmel Guild. Because he embraced the ideas of the young priests during the changes of Vatican Council II, some of his own classmates shunned him.

Be careful when you see a man taking an unorthodox path. He may be as unorthodox as Jesus was.

> As the Father loves me, so I also love you. Remain in my love. —John 15:9

> Let us never seek Christ without the cross.
> —St. John of the Cross

> By slowly converting our loneliness into deep solitude, we create that precious space where we can discover our voice telling us about our inner necessity—that is—our vocation. —Henri Nouwen

160.

But grace was given to each of us according to the measure of Christ's gift. —Ephesians 4:7

My brother,

You are you and I am I. Neither of us can duplicate the other. The measure of God's goodness that has been bestowed on each of us is special to ourselves.

Why then, my friend, should I be envious of you or your talents, or your accomplishments, or even your position in the church?

Jealousy is an evil demon that sometimes enters closed societies such as the priesthood. Men begin to compare their lives, their assignments, their friends, and even their reputations.

How sad! Why would you ever want to be someone else? You are "special to the Lord."

We have much to learn from God's poor. They have nothing. Yet, if you come to know them, each has a dignity that rests within them. That is why so many priests and religious over the years have toiled in areas of poverty, and have been saddened when they were transferred. They came to know and to love God's people. They see and experience God in them.

And you, my friend, look around you. There are people who want your love, who need your care. To them, you are wonderful. To them, you are Christ. Why would you ever want to be someone else?

One of the saddest sights one priest ever encountered occurred in his early days as a priest.

It was at the funeral of a priest. The archbishop was there. He went to the cemetery. As the mourners left the grave and walked back to the cars, two older monsignors walking behind the bishop got into a shoving match. Each was elbowing the other as if they were two schoolboys. Each wanted to be closest to the bishop. To see grown men acting like children trying to get the attention of a superior is a sorry spectacle indeed.

> But by the envy of the devil, death entered into the world, and they who are in his possession experience it.
> —Wisdom 2:24

> Evil is never in things, but in men and their distorted wills. —Frederico Suarez

> The word of God is too sublime to be used by man as a means of self-glorification. —Aloysius Biskupek, S.V.D.

> Sanctity properly consists in simple conformity to the Divine Will expressed in an exact fulfillment of the duties of one's proper state. —Pope Benedict XV

Making the Invisible, Visible:
The Role of the Prophet

161.

Faith is the realization of what is hoped for and evidence of things not seen. —Hebrews 11:1

My brother,

Faith is a light that shines in our darkness. Faith is a pure gift. It comes from God. It enables us to sense the ineffable, the invisible. After all, a priest in his prophetic role is a man who makes the invisible God visible to others through his own life. Our vision, our faith, gives us the ability to manifest to others the wonders and mysteries of God. Every day, our thoughts, words, and deeds are sacramental because the "Holy Presence" is actualized and made present in the world through us.

Do you not realize how terribly essential you are? Your faith is the beacon that shows our people the way to realities that "eyes have not seen, that ears have not heard." Blessed are you!

One great difference between our age and the ages of the past is the impact of the visual and auditory upon people. The television, Internet, and radio literally drown people in images and sound. How can God break through these barriers? Only through God's messengers! Only through us!

> How beautiful upon the mountains
> are the feet of him who brings glad tidings,
> Announcing peace, bearing good news,
> announcing salvation, and saying to Zion,
> "Your God is King!" —Isaiah 52:7

Real discernment is that which sees the infinite distance between the lasting and the transitory. —Gustav Thils

Heralds of the Gospel are expert in humanity, profoundly knowing the heart of contemporary man, who shares his joys and hopes, his fears and sorrows, and, at the same time, who are contemplatives in love with God.
—The Priest and the Third Christian Millennium

The faithful are quick to perceive in a priest the loss of faith in his own priesthood. —Raymond A. Tartre, S.S.S.

The priest possesses a sacredness imminent in his own person, for he sustains a privileged relationship to the Godhead. —Jean Galot, S.J.

162.

And for this reason we too give thanks to God unceasingly, that, in receiving the word of God from hearing us, you received not a human word but, as it truly is, the word of God, which is now at work in you who believe.
—1 Thessalonians 2:13

My brother,
    The "word" of God is active, reaching to the very core of our being. All things are received according to the philosophers in accord with the nature of the one who receives. You, my friend, are a soul who has received the word like an open field. It came upon you, and settled like the dew in the night that softens the ground. It settled into your soul like a field receives seed to produce a harvest.
    How many times did you hear God's word? Suddenly one day, you were filled with certainty. For you, faith became a certain reality. "I am called. I believe. The priesthood is my life, my vocation."
    But we must take care lest our hearts become as hard as the earth in winter.

The seed sown on rocky ground is the one who hears the word and receives it at once with joy. But he has no root and lasts only for a time. When some tribulation or persecution comes because of the word, he immediately falls away. —Matthew 13:20–21

The priest cannot act consistently with what he is unless he lets himself be permeated ever more deeply by the spirit of the gospel. —Jean Galot, S.J.

We need to appreciate that the only way to know God is to proceed with humility, simplicity, and poverty, enter God's silence, and there in patient prayer wait until Divinity reveals itself according to its own good timetable. —Wilkie Au

This discerned art of holiness is not a matter of learning a catalogue of answers and then distributing them on request. —George A. Aschenbrenner, S.J.

You alone are the reader of hearts, O God, and how can I expect to understand the heart of another when I don't even understand my own? —Karl Rahner, S.J.

163.

. . . my just one shall live by faith. —Hebrews 10:38

My brother,

Martin Luther based his whole theology on the above state-ment. Faith, for Martin, trumped all else. It was the very means of salvation. It was the means of grace that carried us home to God.

You live by faith. When you said, "Here I am" to the bishop, you took an irrevocable step in faith. You became "God's man." From that moment on, you were dedicated, consecrated, and set adrift upon the sea of life with only faith to guide you.

Fate maneuvered your life. So you came to be where you stand today. Nothing happened by chance. Perhaps your life seemed to be a gamble, a question of chance. However, it was all programmed from above.

Have you accepted your life? If it gave you lemons, did you make lemonade? If it gave you sweet fruits, did you stop to savor God's goodness to you? Yet, there is still today! And, God willing, there will be a tomorrow.

> LORD, my allotted portion and my cup,
> you have made my destiny secure. —Psalms 16:5

> Think [that] pleasing God is all God cares about. But any fool in the world can see that God is always trying to please us back, always making little surprises and springing them on us when we least expect it.
> —Alice Walker

> There is nothing we should shun more earnestly, after sin, than anxiety. —St. Francis de Sales

> In keeping with the very institution of Christ, the church needs most of all a ministry in which a man surrenders himself totally to the exigencies of his mission. —Jean Galot, S.J.

The priest, in imitation of His High Priest, sanctifies himself for the service of men.
—Raymond A. Tartre, S.S.S.

164.

By faith we understand that the universe was ordered by the word of God, so that what is visible came into being through the invisible. —Hebrews 11:3

My brother,

The cosmos is becoming more apparent to mankind. Our spaceships and telescopes are revealing the length and breadth and height of the universe. Science is unveiling the secrets of the heavens.

But isn't it beautiful that the Creator reveals himself to little ones like us, who can barely comprehend our own small planet? In the deep dark recesses of our soul, the one who created the stars still deigns to speak to us.

We who are trained theologians have the obligation to continually define the invisible Creator with words that our people can understand. Not many are abstract thinkers. Not many of our congregants on Sunday can deal with ideas and concepts. We must put flesh on the invisible. To do that, we need only point to the crucifix. The concept of *"ipsum esse subsistens"* may be beyond most of us. However, the divine Word become flesh is a reality that can move our souls to pure love.

Don't you dread Trinity Sunday? It was a blessing to the priests that ordinations took place on the Saturday before Trinity Sunday. We could preach on the glories of the priesthood. At least the priesthood is something concrete. It is not an abstract idea.

But then, for some reason, the ordination date began to move around. And in some dioceses, there were no new priests.

So we were left with the Trinity. We spoke of Word and Spirit. We used the shamrock. We spoke of the sign of the cross. But somehow, we knew that we were in a land of mystery and the people sat there—believing, yet with blank stares. Raw

theology is tough to preach. Yet, we must do the best we can.
We will understand it in eternity.

> When you lift up the Son of Man, then you will realize
> that I AM. . . . —John 8:28

> The curse of this age is that the Savior of the world is
> not known. —Jacques Millet, S.J.

> It is by no means easy to love something deeply if it is
> only perceived faintly. —Frederico Suarez

> Words move but examples draw. —Pope John XXIII

165.

> *All these died in faith. They did not receive what had been
> promised but saw it and greeted it from afar and
> acknowledged themselves to be strangers and aliens on earth,
> for those who speak thus show that they are seeking a
> homeland.* —Hebrews 11:13, 14

My brother,

A few years ago, the notion of *Heilsgeschichte* (salvation history) was all the rage. But Salvation History is now moving
more and more quickly, and inexorably, to a new stage.

Many religious creeds self-destruct with the passage of time.
They cannot endure the scrutiny of human progress. Islam, for
one, may possibly implode in a detonation that may rock the
world as it makes one final desperate attempt to force the conversion of the world to its ways.

No doubt about it, we are on the brink of apocalyptic times
as we enter the twenty-first century. Not that the world will
end. It will move into a new era. As Peter and the apostles
could not foresee the future, neither can we. But the signs of
the times are all around us. We are at a watershed in history.
We are strangers and foreigners on the earth. Nevertheless, we
are also those who will bring this world to its fulfillment.

It was 1944. I was working in a butcher shop. The boss was out. Suddenly, a rather tattered figure appeared. He had pamphlets in his hand.

"Repent, brother," he said. "The time of dissolution is at hand. The mark of the beast is all around us. Time is short. Give yourself to Jesus."

His spiel lasted five minutes. I stood there transfixed, not knowing what to say. Suddenly, he started all over again. "Repent, brother, the time of dissolution is at hand."

Just then, the boss walked in, went to the cash register, and handed the man a quarter.

"I didn't know what he wanted," I said.

"He just wanted you to buy his pamphlet," said the boss.

I never forgot the man. He was proclaiming the *parousia*— and all for a quarter.

A prophet reads the signs of the times. It is the job of the priest to read the prophet. Do we really understand what people are saying when they speak to us?

> To him who loves us and has freed us from our sins by his blood, who has made us into a kingdom, priests for his God and Father, to him be glory and power forever [and ever]. Amen. —Revelation 1:5, 6

> The powers bestowed upon the priests to be exercised in the name of Christ are divine powers. Thus, the priest emerges as the man of God, the man in whom God acts with special power. —Jean Galot, S.J.

> Our call to the priesthood makes it obligatory to follow in the footsteps of Jesus, our King, and to fight by His side in a war that is both just and honorable.
> —Jacques Millet, S.J.

166.

By faith Abel offered to God a sacrifice greater than Cain's.
Through this he was attested to be righteous, God bearing
witness to his gifts, and through this, though dead, he still
speaks. —Hebrews 11:4

My brother,

According to Saint Paul, Abel's gift to God was more pleasing than his brother's because he offered it with faith. Of course, it was no accident that the Jews were herdsmen, as was Abel, and the Canaanites were farmers, as was Cain. Thus, the Torah is more favorable to the herdsmen. After all, it is the victors who write history. The losers are those about whom the victors write books.

But the point is well taken. Priests must be men of faith. Yes, the liturgy is the church at prayer. Yes, the Holy Sacrifice of the Mass is the work of Christ re-presenting himself to the Father. But nevertheless, the priest who stands in for our Lord needs to approach the sacred mystery with awe. This *"mysterium tremendens et fascinans"* cannot be handled lightly or routinely. It is a power—a *dunamis*—that can shake the universe.

> I will raise the cup of salvation
> and call on the name of the LORD. —Psalms 116:13

> We cannot trifle with something as holy as the body
> and blood of Christ. We cannot play games with the
> Holy of Holies. —Frederico Suarez

> The Mass perpetuates the purest, deepest, and most
> powerful love of God and of man.
> —Aloysius Biskupek, S.V.D.

> Even during a celebration of the Eucharist, he [the
> priest] is also kneeling in his heart. He is also in some
> sense, silently, secretly, hiddenly at one with the laity.
> —Peter Cassarella

Only the ordained priest has received a "special grace" to gather up that offering and present it to the Father as a sacrifice of praise and adoration. This is the element that constitutes the uniqueness of the ordained priesthood. —Raymond A. Tartre, S.S.S.

167.

. . . *who by faith conquered kingdoms, did what was righteous, obtained the promises; they closed the mouths of lions, put out raging fires, escaped the devouring sword; out of weakness they were made powerful, became strong in battle, and turned back foreign invaders. Women received back their dead through resurrection. Some were tortured and would not accept deliverance, in order to obtain a better resurrection. Others endured mockery, scourging, even chains and imprisonment. They were stoned, sawed in two, put to death at sword's point; they went about in skins of sheep or goats, needy, afflicted, tormented. The world was not worthy of them. They wandered about in deserts and on mountains, in caves and in crevices in the earth.*
—Hebrews 11:33–38

My brother,

These ancient heroes conquered their persecutors by faith. Let's be honest. Ordinary people could not endure the above mentioned horrors without divine assistance. Most of us complain if we get so much as a hangnail or stub our toe. Few of us could bear unbearable pain.

Thank God, most of us won't have to undergo the misery that becomes glory in the lives of the martyrs. Our lives, at worst, will be uncomfortable—and, at times, painful, but for the most part bearable.

But why miss the key ingredient? By faith we can conquer all things, even our own insecurity and weakness. We may not be called to be martyrs—but with faith we can endure what the Lord sends us.

One of the great, yet invisible, examples of faith today are those priests—as few or as many as they may be—who have been swept up wrongly in the current priest scandal of pedophilia. They are suffering in silence—in limbo—while they are innocent. God knows their hearts. God knows their faith.

> . . . without me you can do nothing. —John 15:5

> God is the ruler even though the whole world rise up against Him. —Aloysius Biskupek, S.V.D.

> The priest tries to be, in his whole life, a "sacrament" in the broad sense, in order to carry in all his actions a sanctifying converting power. —Gustav Thils

> The priest who is on his knees before the Sacred Tabernacle in a reverent manner and who prays attentively to God is, for the Christian people, an example, offering them an incentive and an invitation to rival such a priest in zealous piety.
> —Pope John XXIII

> How great is the value of converse with Christ [in the eucharist] for there is nothing more consoling on earth, nothing more efficacious for advancing along the road of holiness. —Pope Paul VI

168.

> . . . but only faith working through love. —Galatians 5:6

My brother,

Faith ends up—when it is true faith—in love. It has nowhere else to go.

Faith is not really blind. Faith sees what the world cannot. It sees beauty in ugliness. It can find solace in sorrow. It can be confronted with pain and yet find joy.

Love is the expression of faith. For faith instinctively finds God in all the vicissitudes of life because faith sees the one common factor behind all reality. The face of God may be hidden, but when faith is present, all physical things—all apparent realities—disappear. They become transparent. And the presence of God manifests itself. Faith sees God in every face and every circumstance. And faith begets love.

Dorothy Day is a wonderful model for priestly charity. She and Peter Maurin were constantly surrounded by God's poor. They welcomed each person unconditionally. They saw Christ in their eyes.

Brother, do they come to your parish for food or a handout? If so, do you look in their eyes and see Christ? Or do you let the secretary or cook handle things at the kitchen door?

> Let it be done for you according to your faith.
> —Matthew 9:29

> We will never do justice to the priestly character by conceiving it as a mere capacity to engage in ministerial endeavors. It is first and foremost a relation to God who first, through Christ, and then through priests, seeks to reveal Himself and to bring his own action to bear upon the world. —Jean Galot, S.J.

> Constancy is the perfection of justice; it inspires confidence and gives the priest an irresistible influence over men. —Aloysius Biskupek, S.V.D.

> Prayer means turning to reality, taking over our part, however, humble, tentative, and half understood, in the continual conversation, the communion of our spirits with the eternal Spirit. —Evelyn Underhill

169.

> *Consequently, the law was our disciplinarian for Christ, that*
> *we might be justified by faith. But now that faith has come,*
> *we are no longer under a disciplinarian. For through faith*
> *you are all children of God in Christ Jesus.*
> —Galatians 3:24-26

My brother,

It is nice to belong to a family. It is a great feeling to be part of something bigger than oneself. As sons of God, heirs of heaven, we share a common destiny with the whole of mankind. The kingdom of heaven is among us—and within us.

Paul's reference to the "Law," to the Torah, was because the law was for mankind what a drill sergeant is for new army recruits. He molds them and whips them into true soldiers. They become trained to be disciplined members of a unit— men who will do as they are commanded.

With Christ, we no longer stand as soldiers—subject to an uncaring training. We are sons of God. We understand the Lord as *Abba*, our heavenly Lord—not *Jehovah*, the harsh commander. We act as we do, not out of fear or reverence, but out of filial love.

> Teach me wisdom and knowledge,
> for in your commands I trust. —Psalms 119:66

> That man is an apostle who possesses an apostolic soul.
> —Gustav Thils

> If the essential task of the priest is not only to offer
> sacrifice, but to intercede on behalf of mankind, the
> fundamental intention of love appears more vividly in
> the priesthood. —Jean Galot, S.J.

> Wherever canon laws are multiplied, charity becomes
> extinct. —Anonymous

Everything I have read in my study of the Gospel is
that Jesus wants men and women of heart, not rules.
—Dean Hoge

170.

*... insofar as I now live in the flesh, I live by faith in the Son
of God who has loved me and given himself up for me.*
—Galatians 2:20

My brother,

Paul offers himself time and time again as our model. He so
much wants for his people to have what he has, to know what
he knows. It is the ecstatic joy he experiences that motivates
him.

Over and over, he speaks of the son of God who has loved
him. And again and again, Paul wants to remind us that Christ
loved him so much that he willingly, happily, and without
reservation, gave his life for ours.

It is the life of faith that makes all things possible. It is the
key that opens the door. Faith is the instrument that enables all
of the good things of Christ to become present.

My friend, our life is a life of faith. All the joy and peace that
the church has to offer is ours. All we need to do is express our
"credo"— it is our passport to the joys of Christian being.

In my own lifetime, it has been necessary to undergo a
rethinking of our faith.

Father Shae correctly said that our theology was like a wall
composed of many bricks. Take one out—remove one dogma
or tenet—the whole wall will loosen and crumble.

With the advent of higher criticism in scripture, and a
rethinking of our theology, sure enough the wall came apart.

Miraculously, another wall—a more ancient, more actual,
wall of truth, was revealed standing behind the first one. Praise
God—the church still stands. The cornerstone has not been
removed.

I do believe, help my unbelief! —Mark 9:24

Prayer, then, is the weapon of the priest. A priest who does not pray is but a spent star which no longer gives light, a dried up channel through which water has ceased to flow; a resounding cymbal whose noise tortures the ear without touching the heart.
—Jacques Millet, S.J.

If you are not a man of prayer, I don't believe in the sincerity of your intentions when you say you work for Christ. —The Way

Holy Mass is at the center of my life.
—Pope John Paul II

171.

The aim of this instruction is love from a pure heart, a good conscience, and a sincere faith. —1 Timothy 1:5

My brother,
    The love that Paul describes is what we aim at—not what we have achieved.
    This is the hard part. We preach love and a little voice within us says, "You are not totally pure. You do not have a perfectly good conscience. Your faith may be sincere, but it is very weak." We know what we are. We want to say, with Peter, "Depart from me, Lord, for I am a sinful man" (Lk 5:8).
    But there is another voice, not ours, that says, "You are mine. I have chosen you. All of your faults, weaknesses, and failures were entered into the equation of my love long before you agreed to come to me. There is nothing about you I do not know. There is no weakness that I have not prepared for. I am God."
    So, brother, don't be intimidated. Your weaknesses really don't count, you know. He can more than compensate. He is pure mercy.

Before Vatican Council II, almost every priest I know mumbled his way through the breviary every day. It took about one hour and ten minutes. Somehow, some way, we got it all read by midnight. Of course, in all truth, the intricacies of the Latin language escaped most of us. But we all recited the breviary.

A priest once said at a meeting of priests, "Wouldn't it be great if the breviary were in English? Just think, all of the psalms would be in our brains as we preach."

Then the book went into English. In the late 1970s, the bishop called a convocation. "Bring your breviary," was the order.

Some had to hunt for the book. Some had to go and buy the four volumes. Others had to brush up on how to properly recite the thing. They had not seen it in years.

Brother, look at it this way. When you pray that breviary, you are the whole church lifting your voice to God. You represent your people. It is the community using your voice. Pray it well. It will soothe your soul and fill your heart with God's words.

I cling to your decrees, LORD;
do not let me come to shame.
I will run the way of your commands
for you open my docile heart. —Psalms 119:31–32

To sanctify your clergy, get your priests to recite the Divine Office with attention, and to celebrate Mass with devotion. These exercises are enough to make them perfect. —St. Joseph of Cupertino

Pour out upon these, thy servants, the blessing of the Holy Spirit and the power of thy priestly grace. Sustain them forever with the bounty of thy gifts. —Roman Ritual, Ordination Prayer

For any mature experience of sorrow, we must know that we are genuinely responsible for our sin. —George A. Aschenbrenner, S.J.

172.

. . . for, if you confess with your mouth that Jesus is Lord and believe in your heart that God raised him from the dead, you will be saved. For one believes with the heart and so is justified, and one confesses with the mouth and so is saved.
—Romans 10:9, 10

My brother,

Heart and lips are the two components of our prayer life. However, for our lives to be totally integral, the expressions of our lips must totally reflect the sentiments of our hearts.

Externally, on the altar and in our daily service to the community, we are forever making pronouncements about the divine will. Many times, we speak as if we were the total reflection of the divine will. We, throughout our priestly lives, interpret God's written word for the world around us. For some priests, their lives are spent making pronouncements.

How sad it would be, therefore, if we were to be divided internally. It is not possible for us to speak honestly if our faith is empty. It must be that, from our heart, our faith will break forth and the mouth will speak the word of salvation for our people. We will sing God's praises every day, but only if our voices are like those of nature—pure in our praise of God.

It's easy to speak about God's will. It is more difficult to accept it.

One of the best, happiest, and holiest priests in the 1940s received a change of assignment. He went from a warm, loving, happy parish to one of the worst situations in the diocese. It was a situation where the parish secretary literally ran the parish. She owned the pastor. She controlled the rectory. She monitored the single phone line. She controlled the societies. She made life miserable for the curates. The people themselves complained to the archbishop. Nothing happened. Dozens of priests left the parish.

Our happy, holy priest endured it all. He conquered by his goodness. Actually, he died in that assignment. He is honored to this day. The pastor and the secretary are forgotten.

Lord, open my lips;
my mouth will proclaim your praise. —Psalms 51:17

Who does not know that teaching is almost worthless if the priest does not confirm by his example that which he delivers by word. —Pope Pius X

Preachers who do not live holy lives are like road signs which point out the right way to others, but themselves remain in the same place immovably. —St. Augustine

Every preacher should know his own flock well and use an attractive style which, rather than wounding people, strikes the conscience and is not afraid to call things for what they are. —Cardinal Ratzinger

173.

In all circumstances, hold faith as a shield, to quench all [the] flaming arrows of the evil one. —Ephesians 6:16

My brother,
Faith comes to us as a pure gift. It is our protector against the wiles and snares of our enemies. It will ward off attacks of gloom, and the insidious little doubts that can cause us so much damage.

How many of our priests go through long periods of insecurity? In the darkness, we can only exclaim with more hope than certainty, "The LORD is my light and my salvation" (Ps 27:1).

We are truly armed with the helmet of salvation. Baptism has created an aura—a helmet if you want—that guards our minds from the blows of fear and doubt. There is no power on earth or in hell that can take away or destroy your own reality or your Catholic identity.

Moreover, as a priest, the Holy Spirit is at your service. Do you actually believe that you live and operate on your own? My friend, you are a terror for the enemies of Christ. You see yourself as a simple priest. The enemy trembles at your approach. You are armed with and protected by the power of God. You are invincible.

Before the changes that transformed our seminaries, the seminarians were drilled in book theology. Tomes by Herve, Noldin, Schmidt, and Tanquerey presented propositions that were backed up by church teaching, scripture, tradition, and reason. The prime task for the student was to memorize. In effect, by ordination, every priest was a "walking catechism," ready to teach as well as defend "the faith."

After Vatican Council II, the theology books were gone. Book theology was dismissed. Our new men moved into truly academic curricula, with core courses and electives. The result has been mixed. Why? Because, to be honest, the quality of teaching has been mixed. The reality is that some priests don't completely know the faith, nor can they fully explain the faith. The vast majority are, of course, probably better educated than those of us who came before. But brother, you cannot stop reading as soon as you are ordained.

When Gertrude Stein was dying, she is supposed to have asked, "If these are the answers, what were the questions?" Do you know the questions of today?

> He put on justice as his breastplate,
> salvation, as the helmet on his head;
> He clothed himself with garments of vengeance,
> wrapped himself in a mantle of zeal. —Isaiah 59:17

> Faith strips the mask from the world and reveals God in everything. —Charles de Foucauld

> The priest is a different kind of presence in the world. —Bishops' Committee for Priestly Life and Ministry

> It is not enough to stop at what we once learned in the seminary. . . . The process of intellectual formation must last all of one's life. —Cardinal Ratzinger

An Anchor in the Storm:
Hope as a Stable Force in Our Life

174.

For in hope we were saved. Now hope that sees for itself is not hope. For who hopes for what one sees? But if we hope for what we do not see, we wait with endurance.
—Romans 8:24, 25

My brother,

Faith and hope correspond to each other. Both involve the "not yet," that which is not apparent. It is faith in Jesus Christ and his mercy that undergirds both our faith and our hope.

The Christian life itself is apparent only through the words, deeds, and character of Christians. It is not theoretical—a series of abstractions that have no consequences. Christians are sustained in faith and hope by the reality of God's gifts within them. Nourished and motivated by word and sacrament, Christ becomes present in the soul.

Brother, stay close to the Lord by daily prayer. Nourished by the bread of life and the cup of salvation, every day will bring optimism. The invisible, hope, will be so tangible that every day will be spent in the presence of God.

Theological hope is very different from just hope. Every week, I take a lottery ticket. Every week, I hope to win. So far, as they say in Vegas, "it's good I have bad luck, or I wouldn't have any luck at all."

Our faith is like the beacon from the lighthouse. It shows us that the firm shore is ahead. It leads us home. Hope is the absolute certainty that somehow, some way, we will make it home.

My soul rests in God alone,
from whom comes my salvation.
God alone is my rock and salvation,
my secure height; I shall never fall. —Psalms 62:2–3

The minister responds to events not by merely
consulting with his own personal propensities, but in
keeping with the mysterious image of the Lord that he
carries within himself. —Jean Galot, S.J.

Settle yourself in solitude and you will come upon Him
in yourself. —St. Teresa of Avila

But if You were not incomprehensible, You would be
inferior to me, for my mind could grasp and assimilate
You. You would belong to me, instead of I to You.
—Karl Rahner, S.J.

175.

*For here we have no lasting city, but we seek the one that is
to come.* —Hebrews 13:14

My brother,

The above statement means very little to young priests. We
are filled with life and energy. Every day brings new challenges. Our bodies are generally strong and healthy. It seems
that nothing can change, nor that life will end—or at least end
soon.

But as we get older, our perspective, of necessity, begins to
change. The landscape all around us begins to change. Family
and friends disappear. The man in the looking glass slowly
changes. Hair thins, wrinkles appear, aches and pains begin to
affect us. Our step is slower. We are not as foolish or as gullible
as we once were.

As we see younger men take the posts of the priests of our
youth, we cannot avoid the reality. The city of man is no lasting place. Time, the measure of motion, is taking its toll.

So now is the time to lift up our eyes to the dawn. We must begin to experience a new joy—a new anticipation. Our true home—our heavenly Jerusalem—lies just over the horizon. All our destiny is there.

> There is an appointed time for everything,
> and a time for every affair under the heavens.
> —Ecclesiastes 3:1

> Poverty of spirit is the meeting place of heaven and earth, the mysterious place where God and we encounter each other, the point where infinite mystery meets concrete existence. —Joannes Metz

> Things are often possessed in ownership and a man then thinks himself free. But he only experiences that [freedom] when he is forced to give them up.
> —Devotio Moderna

> Out of the darkness of my life, so much frustrated, I put before you the one great thing to love on earth—the Blessed Sacrament. . . . There you will find the romance, glory, honor, fidelity, and the true way of all your loves on earth, and more than that: Death: by the divine paradox that which ends life, and demands the surrender of all, and yet by the taste (or foretaste) of which alone can what you seek in your earthly relationships (love, faithfulness, joy) be maintained, or take on that complexion of reality, of eternal endurance, which every man's heart desires. —J.R.R. Tolkien

176.

If for this life only we have hoped in Christ, we are the most pitiable people of all. —1 Corinthians 15:19

My brother,

Herein lies the core of our priestly philosophy. We have, by accepting the priesthood, rejected the world and all its allurements.

How sad, then, when a priest, who has vowed to follow the simple Jesus who had "nowhere to rest his head" (Mt 8:20), begins to wonder, "What shall I eat? What shall I wear?" How easy it is to take advantage of the priesthood.

How often do we, like the Pharisees, demand "the first seats in the synagogue" and "want to be addressed as 'Rabbi'?" We begin to expect the respect of men and deference to our clerical position.

As years go by, how easy to look for a better parish, an easier assignment, or a more prestigious post.

If you want a true meditation on worldly honor, then visit the Cathedral. Consider the men who once wore bishop's attire and who now rest in the crypt below. Many of them were holy. But, if they were not, what did their position avail them?

> For where your treasure is, there also will your heart be. —Luke 12:34

> What is happiness but the love and possession of the sovereign good? —John Nicholas Grou, S.J.

> The Lord does not ask us to be successful. He asks us to be faithful. —Mother Teresa

> It is hard for a man who is ever being praised and flattered not to give in to thoughts of personal pride and not to accept his due, the honors with which he is surrounded. —Raymond A. Tartre, S.S.S.

177.

For we know that if our earthly dwelling, a tent, should be destroyed, we have a building from God, a dwelling not made with hands, eternal in heaven. —2 Corinthians 5:1

My brother,

How lofty is the ideal of the perfect resignation on earth that is joined to fervent faith and hope in eternal life.

All of us believe fervently in our divine creator, and in our ultimate destiny. Faith impels us. Hope sustains us. And love guides us.

Nevertheless, we are natural. The visible and the tangible are very conformable to our nature. The invisible and the spiritual are much more difficult.

Yet, as priests, our role is to make the invisible visible to those to whom we are sent. For example, in the grief and sorrow of the loss of a loved one, how comforting it is for the family to hear the quiet confidence of the priest as he paints a beautiful picture of that place of light, happiness, and peace. It is your confidence, my friend, that bolsters and supports so many who have lost the vision of God. You are the visionary who helps the blind to see.

How comforting it is for the people to hear the priest say or sing these words of the Preface that, for their loved one, "life is changed not ended." Our Catholic vision of eternal life is so necessary for their peace of soul. And for those who have lost that vision, you, oh priest, are the one whose job it is to restore the vision—to hold out hope.

> Then the angel said to me, "Write this! Blessed are those who have been called to the wedding feast of the Lamb." —Revelation 19:9

The priest does not merely officiate at a ceremony. He presides over the participation of this community of people in the death and resurrection of Christ and their access through Christ to the Father and to each other, their being one with each other in Christ and in Spirit.
—Bishops' Committee for Priestly Life and Ministry

Oh, what a sad and deplorable sight it would be if we had the eyes of our mind opened to see the priest touching divine mysteries surrounded on every side by choirs of angels, struck with awe, and yet, the priest is utterly cold, and, as if stupid, pays no attention to what he does, does not understand what he says, and thus hastens on to the end, confusing signs and rushing over words so that he seems not to know what he is doing.
—St. Gregory the Great

Through my own attitude, I can transform the holiest events into the gray tedium of dull routine. My days don't make me dull. It is the other way around.
—Karl Rahner, S.J.

178.

For the grace of God has appeared, saving all and training us to reject godless ways and worldly desires and to live temperately, justly, and devoutly in this age, as we await the blessed hope, the appearance of the glory of the great God and of our savior Jesus Christ. . . . —Titus 2:11–13

My brother,
We are trained by the church to be a "contradiction" to the world. The priest is the agent of the divine in the economy of salvation. He is asked to be a light shining upon a hill, a stable rock in an unstable world. We are the good stewards going about the Lord's business taking care of the household of God until he comes. Day by day, week by week, God asks one thing—that we be faithful, that we be steady.

Jesus has said that when he comes, and if he finds his servants waiting, he will gird himself and wait on his servants. Outside, in the world, in the kingdom of the secular, there is turmoil, division, passion, and strife. Inside God's house, that is, the church, the kingdom of God, tranquility must reign. It is a kingdom of love, peace, and sacrifice. We must keep all things peacefully in order until the bridegroom arrives. One of the great gifts of the holy liturgy prior to Vatican Council II was the great hushed silence of the Mass.

My brother, who had many children, said, "How I used to look forward to Mass on Sunday. Just for an hour, I could enjoy the peace of church. Now, they have us singing and jumping up and down. Loudspeakers blast the sermon in my ears. Even the Mass parts are noisy. I miss the peace."

Perhaps, brother, we need to examine our liturgy to see if it is too frenetic—too packed with noise and activity. Do your parishioners sense the mystery of God on the Lord's day?

> Who, then, is the faithful and prudent servant, whom the master has put in charge of his household to distribute to them their food at the proper time? Blessed is that servant whom his master on his arrival finds doing so. —Matthew 24:45-46

> He who pledges himself to work for Christ should never have a free moment, because to rest is not to do nothing, it is to relax in activities that require less effort. —Frederico Suarez

> Prayer is not recreation; it requires the application of mental and bodily faculties, the expenditure of bodily strength and energy. —Aloysius Biskupek, S.V.D.

> Being up-in-arms about everyone and everything contaminates the ground of the soul and turns it into barren land. —Cardinal Ratzinger

179.

. . . and hope does not disappoint. . . . —Romans 5:5

My brother,

The author Charles Peguy, a Catholic who loved God so much, but who, due to circumstances in his life, was prevented from entering into full communion with the church, was in love with the virtue of hope. He wrote a long poem in which he described hope in many ways.

One of those was to speak of hope as a little girl. Her older sisters are faith and charity. And, in his poem, Charles has God speak as follows.

The faith that I love best, says God, is hope,
Faith doesn't surprise me.
It's not surprising.
I am so resplendent in my creation.
That, in order really not to see me, these poor people
would have to be blind.

Charity doesn't surprise me.
It's not surprising.
These poor creatures are so miserable that, unless they
had a heart of stone,
How could they not have love for one another?
How could they not love their brothers?
How could they not take the bread from their own
mouth, their daily bread,
In order to give it to the unhappy children who pass
by?
And my son had such love for them.

But hope, says God, that is something that surprises
me. Even me.
That is surprising.

That these poor children see how things are going, and
   believe that tomorrow things will go better.
That they see how things are going today, and believe
   that they will go better tomorrow morning.
This is surprising, and it's by far the greatest marvel of
   our grace,
And I'm surprised by it myself.
And my grace must indeed be an incredible force.

My friend, "Trust in the Lord!" (Ps 37:3). Things will go better tomorrow.

The hungry he has filled with good things;
the rich he has sent away empty. —Luke 1:53

People need to feel that they are not alone, that they are
not unknown, that they are not without meaning.
—Bishops' Committee on Priestly Life and Ministry

You have made me your priest, and thus have chosen
me to be an earthly sign of your grace to others. You
have put your grace into my hands, your truth into my
mouth. —Karl Rahner, S.J.

The priest himself needs the community he serves.
—Bishops' Committee on Priestly Life and Ministry

180.

*This we have as an anchor of the soul, sure and firm, which
reaches into the interior behind the veil. . . .* —Hebrews 6:19

My brother,
   The anchor is a fitting symbol for hope. Like a ship, we are
subject to life's variable currents. At times, we find ourselves in
calm waters. All is peaceful. The sun shines. The sea of our life
is like a glass surface without wave or ripple.
   But often trouble clouds our sky. Our world becomes dark.
Waves of trouble dash against us. We find ourselves in a sea of

troubles. If the storm is serious enough, we wonder if we can survive, spiritually, emotionally, and even physically.

The only anchor we have is our hope—our trust bolstered by faith that this too will pass. We need sometimes to hear the voice of Jesus. It is his voice that we hear in the gospel. But we need to listen.

Take courage, it is I, do not be afraid! —Mark 6:50

In adverse and difficult times, show a broad back through patient strength and tranquility of soul. Preserve a good heart through trust in God.
—Lord Dirk of Herxen

While the priest is an ordinary man, he has been called by Christ to bear an extraordinary message, to carry on Christ's mission, to teach Christ's truth, to shepherd God's people.
—Declaration on Priestly Life and Ministry

Do not get anxious when the waves batter against your boat; have no fear while God is with you.
—St. Francis de Sales

Be now the God of my hope. —Karl Rahner, S.J.

I've had many troubles in my life—but most of them never happened. —Mark Twain

181.

He [Abraham] believed, hoping against hope, that he would become "the father of many nations," according to what was said, "Thus shall your descendants be." . . . That is why "it was credited to him as righteousness." —Romans 4:18, 22

My brother,

Saint Paul was fighting a reversion by some Christians back to Jewish laws. So, he goes back, not to Moses, but to the Patriarch—to the beginning, to the friend of God, Abraham.

Abram heard a voice. Abram believed. Abram left his home and followed the voice of God. Though childless, he believed when he was told that he would have a land, and a progeny more numerous than the stars.

All of his hopes were ultimately fulfilled. So, Saint Paul presents him to us. Faith and hope are gifts from God. If we accept them fully, then we shall be like Abraham, the friend of God.

We priests can become "Abraham," the father of a multitude, not by carnal nature, but in our spiritual sons and daughters— those who believe in God through us. And they, our children in Christ, will be accredited to us as a pledge of our own justice.

> I am God the Almighty. Walk in my presence and be blameless. —Genesis 17:1

> Dearest brother, be mature and not light in your manner, especially around secular folk, because foolish manners and too many words ill become spiritual men. —Devotio Moderna

> The priestly character impresses upon the being of a baptized person an orientation which commits the whole self to the mission of the priest. God engraves that mission in the very person. He makes it inseparable from personal being. —Jean Galot, S.J.

> Your priest does not approach men as a revivalist or an enthusiast, not as a purveyor of mystic wisdom or gnostic or pentecostal prophet, or whatever else such men may call themselves. These men can communicate to others no more of You than they have themselves. But as a priest, I come as Your legate, as a messenger sent by Your Son, our Lord. And that is at the same time less and more, a thousand times more than anything else. —Karl Rahner, S.J.

182.

*May the God of hope fill you with all joy and peace in
believing, so that you may abound in hope by the power of
the holy Spirit.* —Romans 15:13

My brother,
   If God is with us, who can be against us? If God is the source
of our hope, how can hope fail us? We have support in reserve.
We have resources that defy comprehension.
   Priests, of necessity, need hope. We deal day to day with
intangibles. The product that we sell is no less than eternal life
in God. Yet, we deal with a humanity that is so reliant on the
five senses that our message will seem to many to be nothing
but an illusion.
   Discouragement is so easy. To radiate optimism and a positive message can be enervating—even exhausting. There are
nights after a long day filled with disappointments and trials
when a priest might want to just sit back and lose himself in
anything that brings a little relief. Frankly, God's people can be
so difficult at times that you could wonder why God bothered
to create us at all.
   But just when we have reached that last exasperating point,
something happens. A peace comes from somewhere and we
relax. There is a new day tomorrow. And God knows, somehow, some way, it will all go well—at least, most of it.

   I will not leave you orphans; I will come to you.
   —John 14:18

   Communion is the nature of ultimate reality.
   —Catherine Mowray Lacugna

   Three principal goods are patience, trust, and
   sufficiency. Patience produces trust, trust happiness,
   and sufficiency or contentment the work of grace.
   —Devotio Moderna

I must do all my work with religious care, but without in any way disturbing the tranquility of my soul. I will do just what I can. —Pope John XXIII

183.

. . . but now made manifest through the appearance of our savior Christ Jesus, who destroyed death and brought life and immortality to light through the gospel, for which I was appointed preacher and apostle and teacher. On this account I am suffering these things; but I am not ashamed, for I know him in whom I have believed and am confident that he is able to guard what has been entrusted to me until that day.
—2 Timothy 1:10–12

My brother,

What an amazing calling we have! Imagine, to be a preacher, an apostle, and a teacher is a calling far beyond the ability of any one man. To preach is to stand before the world and to announce Jesus Christ. The kerygma is yours to give.

To be an apostle is to have a mission. You have been sent— commissioned by Christ through his church to represent him to the world.

To be a teacher moves you into the catechetical world. You are to explain diligently and carefully those things taught by the Holy Spirit through the prophets and evangelists.

My brother, you have power. You are, within your own sphere of influence, to make Christ present to the faithful, and even to those who do not know him.

One of the most powerful, most persuasive, and most charismatic preachers who ever lived was—Adolf Hitler.

Monsignor George Shae, as a seminarian, sat in the stadium in Munich in the 1930s at a mass rally early in Hitler's career. He despised all that Hitler represented. Yet, he told me that the crowds, the music, and the hysteria was so great that, when Hitler moved into his power-charged speech, the young student, George Shae, had all he could do to remain sitting. He was caught up in the mass hysteria.

Brother, the purveyor of lies and evil can do much to move people. But you, the minister of life, love, and truth have so much more to give.

What a beautiful calling!

> . . . teaching them to observe all that I have commanded you. And behold, I am with you always, until the end of the age. —Matthew 28:20

> It is not the institution or structure [of society] that the priest has to transform, but the people and they themselves will do the rest. —Frederico Suarez

> What is greater than to direct souls, to fashion the lives of the young? In truth, I consider him greater than any painter or sculptor who knows how to educate the young. —St. John Chrysostom

> And your light continues to shine forth, changing the dark shadows of our earth into the brilliant noon day of your grace, even when this light has to find its way to men through the cracked and dusty panes of my tiny lantern. —Karl Rahner, S.J.

184.

For I am already being poured out like a libation, and the time of my departure is at hand. I have competed well; I have finished the race; I have kept the faith. From now on the crown of righteousness awaits me, which the Lord, the just judge, will award to me on that day, and not only to me, but to all who have longed for his appearance. —2 Timothy 4:6–8

My brother,

Saint Paul has come to the end of his journey. He can now look back over the road he has traveled. With great satisfaction, he can say, "I have kept the faith."

Isn't that our hope and desire? Won't we be happy one day to be able to say to the Lord, "I have accomplished all you gave me to do"?

Oh, make no mistake. You will never be so satisfied that you will be able to say you have accomplished, in earthly terms, all that you could have done. Oh, no, my friend, no man will ever accomplish everything.

But you have tried. You have stayed the course. You have tended to your small plot in the Lord's vineyard. The crown will be yours.

> Rejoice and be glad, for your reward will be great in heaven. —Matthew 5:12

> Only God renders an absolute simple and decisive judgment on things, situations, and persons.
> —Gustav Thils

> O priest, who are you? Not through yourself, for you are drawn from nothing. Not for yourself, since you are a mediator of humanity. Not to yourself, for you are married to the church. Not your own, for you are the servant of all. You are not you, for you are God. Who are you, then? You are nothing and everything.
> —St. Norbert

When I look back in this way, I see my life as a long
highway filled by a column of marching men. Every
moment someone breaks out of the line and goes off
silently, without a word or wave of farewell, to be
swiftly enwrapped in the darkness of the night
stretching out on both sides of the road. . . . True, there
are many others who travel the same road, but only a
few are traveling with me. For the only ones making
this pilgrimage with me are those with whom I set out
together, the ones who were with me at the very start of
my journey to You, my God, the dear ones who were,
and still are, close to my heart. . . . The others are mere
companions of the road, who happen to be going the
same way as I. —Karl Rahner, S.J.

THE PRIESTLY HEART:
A CERTAIN KIND OF LOVE

185.

. . . and that Christ may dwell in your hearts through faith; that you, rooted and grounded in love, may have strength to comprehend with all the holy ones what is the breadth and length and height and depth. . . . —Ephesians 3:17, 18

My brother,

No human can possibly comprehend fully the immensity of love that our Lord holds for us. How can the finite embrace the infinite? How can imperfect human beings even begin to understand the fullness of divine compassion that would urge Jesus Christ to completely abase himself for weak sinful creatures?

No, we cannot take within ourselves a complete realization of the effusion of love. But what we can do is at least begin to try to appreciate the immensity of the gift.

Again, "deep calls to deep" (Ps 42:8). The endless depth of God's perfect charity calls upon the very depth of our soul's being. "I am love. Give me your heart."

But, my friend, one must be prudent. So many priests, in the turbulent days before and after Vatican Council II, gave themselves so totally, that there was nothing left. Many tried to give a complete love to the apostolate.

Thus it was that the expression grew up among us that the "best" priests were leaving the priesthood. For many, their lives became a holocaust for the demands of the people never quit. They come and come and come. Like the waves of the ocean, they and their demands are endless.

Love, without a guide, becomes a runaway train that can only end in the wreckage of a life.

Beloved, if God so loved us, we also must love one another. —1 John 4:11

Late have I loved thee. —St. Augustine

Renew in their hearts the spirit of holiness. —Roman Pontifical, Ordination Prayer

My God and my all. —St. Francis of Assisi

It is very easy for busy priests to slide into a runaway, unfocused rush of daily activities, but how this furthers God's reign of love in the hearts of people can be highly suspect. —George A. Aschenbrenner, S.J.

186.

. . . knowledge inflates with pride, but love builds up.
—1 Corinthians 8:1

My brother,

Saint Paul is speaking about human "knowledge," which is often not knowledge, but a delusion.

Over the years, how many men and women have become infatuated with concepts, ideas, and theories that have led to disaster? How many political, scientific, and social theories have gone terribly wrong?

Ultimately, truth reveals itself. Falsehood always becomes exposed. The so-called "wise" men of the world often end up in the junk bin of history. Their ego trips lead to no place.

But charity—rooted in Christ—is never deceptive. It does not inflate a person's ego. It brings reality. It brings a humility that is truth.

That is why the wise man is always watchful, lest he fall into the trap of unreality. Jesus Christ is pure love, pure truth, and pure humility.

. . . for whoever is begotten by God conquers the world. And the victory that conquers the world is our faith. —1 John 5:4

The priest must behave in an authority which is of a different kind than the social prestige attached to a profession. He must be convinced that his ministry is beneficial for the supernatural well-being of mankind, even if many do not see it that way. —Jean Galot, S.J.

If you are wise, be a reservoir, not a conduit. Be yourself full of what you preach and do not think it enough to pour it out for others. Today in the church we have a profusion of conduits, but how few are the reservoirs. —St. Bernard

This is the height of philosophy, to be simple with prudence. —Pope John XXIII

Knowledge seems more like a kind of pain-killing drug that I have to take repeatedly against the boredom and desolation of my heart. . . . All it can give me is words and concepts, which perform the middleman's service of expressing and interpreting reality to me, but can never still my heart's craving for the reality itself, for true life and true possession. . . . Truly, my God, mere knowing is nothing. —Karl Rahner, S.J.

187.

Rather, living the truth in love, we should grow in every way into him who is the head, Christ. . . . —Ephesians 4:15

My brother,

Speaking the truth in love is sometimes difficult. Why? Because we priests are called upon to speak the truth, which is often rejected by those to whom we speak. Thus, speaking the truth can be fairly easy. But to speak it in charity to those who reject us, our message, and often Jesus Christ himself, is most difficult.

But our efforts to evangelize are never in vain. We never know what flows from our message. And even if it does nothing for those who reject us, the message returns to us. We grow into Christ.

After a period, we will be mature. Others will see the image of Christ in us. "They will look up and see no longer us—but only Jesus" (Cardinal Newman).

However, growth is not mere knowledge. It is a process. Some men simply grow older. They do not grow spiritually or in wisdom.

I well remember a priest sitting in the sacristy, smoking a cigar, the *Daily News* in his hands. Since this was fifteen minutes before Mass, I could presume he was not engaged in meditation. Later on in the day, the same man could be found in his room, the air conditioner on, a gin and tonic in his hand, as he watched the Yankees. The interesting thing was this. He also had the breviary in his other hand. At least he said the office.

He lived. He served. Eventually, he died. He was an adequate priest. I doubt that he moved many souls.

> We belong to God, and anyone who knows God listens to us. . . . —1 John 4:6

> I am a Christian. I am a cleric. I must always and in all my actions represent Jesus Christ, since, as St. Gregory Nazianzen says, priests are clothed in Christ.
> —Pope John XXIII

> One who does not seek the cross of Jesus is not seeking the glory of Jesus. —St. John of the Cross

> The sacristy priest is no longer a reality in America.
> —Raymond A. Tartre, S.S.S.

188.

Owe nothing to anyone, except to love one another; for the one who loves another has fulfilled the law. —Romans 13:8

My brother,

It is hard for a priest to stay out of debt. I don't mean the form of debt that comes from borrowing. We should, of course, avoid spending beyond our means. We should never borrow what we cannot repay.

However, the simple fact is this. People love their priests. People want to do things for the priest. They desire to give things to the priest. They will put themselves out for priests.

Over the course of time, every priest has a long list of people who have been kind to him. We are in a sense debtors to their charity.

The only response that is adequate is our gratitude, our prayers, and our respect. All of that can be summed up in the one word—our love. Be generous with love. Do not forget to do good to those who do good to you. It is an obligation. And there is also an obligation not to take advantage of goodness.

There was a priest who came from poor beginnings. He came to a middle-class parish. One older woman, a widow, took a liking to him.

Soon there were gifts. They were small at first. Then one day, money for a suit. In time, a car followed. Then an expensive ring. Soon this woman, a widow, had poured a fortune into the priest. They traveled to Europe together.

Before it was over, the woman had foolishly gone through her savings.

Then the priest left the parish. She died a few years later, broken-hearted and alone.

Brothers, we cannot allow ourselves to become parasites on the flock. It is rare that it happens. But when it does, it is a scandal.

A brother is a better defense than a strong city. . . .
—Proverbs 18:19

A priest cannot achieve his end, human or supernatural, in isolation. We have only to remember that Our Lord was not a recluse who wanted to avoid contact with his fellow men. —Frederico Suarez

The most deadly poison of our time is indifference. —St. Maximilian Kolbe

Our pastoral activity requires that we should be close to people and all their problems, whether these problems be personal, family, or social ones, but it also demands that we be close to these problems in a priestly way. —Pope John Paul II

189.

. . . and live in love, as Christ loved us and handed himself over for us as a sacrificial offering to God for a fragrant aroma. —Ephesians 5:2

My brother,

Saint Paul gives us a beautiful image here. How many priests would ever believe that their lives were an odor of sweetness, *in odorem suavitatis*, before Almighty God—an offering and a sacrifice to the Lord.

Yet, walking in love is precisely what so many of our priests do. Yes, many seem gruff and many appear to be harsh. Many have problems and many lack a pleasing manner. Many are too intent on "doing the job." Others seem too careless and light-hearted to be sincere about their mission.

But when all is said and done, most are giving of themselves—and are pouring out their lives day by day, year by year. Their gift is their presence. Like the sanctuary lamp, their lives burn day and night before the Lord.

Let me give the example of three priests in one rectory. The "knights of the road"—the handouts—were numerous. It was a city parish.

One priest would smile, be gracious, and hand the guy at the door a quarter.

One would be fairly civil, but give a dollar.

The last priest would scold and lecture the poor bum, and then empty out his pockets.

Pretty soon, the brothers knew which priest to look for. His bark was worse than his bite, and the rewards for listening were ample. However, sometimes the generous priest really hurt feelings.

Wouldn't it be best if we were all pleasant—and generous as well.

> One thing I ask of the LORD;
> this I seek:
> To dwell in the LORD's house
> all the days of my life. . . . —Psalms 27:4

> May he be faithful.
> —Roman Pontifical, Prayer of Consecration

> Ministry means a service, a service whose definitive model is to be found in the Savior of mankind.
> —Jean Galot, S.J.

> God does not consider the number of my deeds, but the way in which I do them; it is the heart he asks for, nothing more. —Pope John XXIII

> God intends a unique imitation of Jesus on the part of every one of us. —George A. Aschenbrenner, S.J.

190.

. . . love one another with mutual affection. . . .
—Romans 12:10

My brother,

If there is any phrase in all of Saint Paul's writings that applies to priests, this is it.

We are the greatest fraternity in the world. There is not now, nor has there ever been, anything else quite like the presbyterate of the Catholic church.

Formerly, because of our rigorous and almost monastic seminary training, the support of the priests for one another was almost tangible. If a priest was ill, the brothers came. If one died, the church was full.

Now, however, in all truth, since Vatican Council II, the ties that bind us have been somewhat weakened. Priests still have priest friends. There are still support groups.

But after a while, that immediate bond of recognition and brotherhood is not always found when priest meets priest. My friend, when did you last contact a sick priest, a retired priest, or go to a priest's funeral?

> Woe to the solitary man! For if he should fall, he has no one to lift him up. —Ecclesiastes 4:10

> Is there anyone who can get by without the help of someone else? Is there anyone in the world who is really self-sufficient? —Frederico Suarez

> By making a decision for celibacy, a man commits himself to a deeper and more universal love.
> —Jean Galot, S.J.

> All priests feel the need for the fellowship of priestly brotherhood and wise ones seek it as best they can.
> —George A. Aschenbrenner, S.J.

The brethren in the presbyterate should always be the special object of the priest's pastoral charity . . . [especially] by affording the opportunity for confession and spiritual direction.
—The Priest and the Third Christian Millennium

191.

. . . your surplus at the present time should supply their needs, so that their surplus may also supply your needs, that there may be equality. As it is written:

"Whoever had much did not have more, and whoever had little did not have less."
—2 Corinthians 8:14, 15

My brother,

In almost all of Paul's letters, he ends by begging for money for needy communities. In fact, Paul was probably one of the great fundraisers of all time. He extracted alms from essentially poor communities.

One of the most irksome and difficult aspects of the priesthood is precisely the need to ask for donations. Some priests are great fundraisers, but most of us groan when a letter comes from the bishop asking for more money to help some cause.

And it never ends. There is always some need, or some diocesan appeal. Or, if you are in a religious order, an appeal may be made for the missions or the mother house.

My friend, take it all in stride. Look around you. See the church throughout the world. On one hand, we build rectories, churches, schools, and convents. In some places, we provide hospitals and orphanages. And always there are the poor.

The Lord will reward you. He has already rewarded the millions since Saint Paul who have gone hat in hand to plead for God's people. It is not easy. But it is part of our Christian mission.

The poor you will always have with you. . . .
—Matthew 26:11

Just as Jesus took upon Himself the miseries of all
mankind, so also the priest, as *"ipse Christus"* is praying
for the community. He takes upon himself the duty of
speaking for all the community.
—Frederico Suarez

The Catholic priesthood possesses the most sublime
and magnificent power on earth. They are depositories
of a great moral force that can move the world.
—Jacques Millet, S.J.

Isn't my heart weak and miserable enough with its own
troubles, without adding to it the crushing woes of
others? —Karl Rahner, S.J.

192.

*Consider this: whoever sows sparingly will also reap
sparingly, and whoever sows bountifully will also reap
bountifully. Each must do as already determined, without
sadness or compulsion, for God loves a cheerful giver.*
—2 Corinthians 9:6, 7

My brother,
   This passage does not usually apply to priests, if we are
speaking of money. Most priests are generous beyond what is
required.
   But, when we come to service—or time—or effort, then we
have a different story.
   After a few years in the priesthood, it becomes more and
more difficult to spend and be spent for the ministry. We simply grow tired.
   Then, when the bell or phone rings, or when people accost
us with requests, that is when our patience wears thin. To be a
cheerful giver of ourselves at all times and in all places is a
superhuman feat of holiness.

How many of us groan inwardly as we are called to one more sick person, or to listen to one more marriage problem, or to endure one more unreasonable demand from a prospective bride. Give what you can, friend—Jesus had the same problem. It is not uncharitable to avoid, for example, a person to whom you have spoken, and who comes back again and again with the same story. If a person is mentally ill—it is simple prudence to avoid him or her. Otherwise, you could yourself be driven to distraction. Every parish has them. If they are "off their medication," you are not going to help. Let the psychiatrist handle the problem.

But be careful. The one person we avoid may be precisely the one who needs us the most.

The crowds went looking for him. . . . —Luke 4:42

The clerical office if only performed carelessly, stands before God as something most miserable, sad, and damnable. —Jacques Millet, S.J.

"Sacerdotem etenim oportet praeesse"—For it is fitting that the priest be in charge. It is necessary, therefore for the priest to have charge, to direct, to watch, to defend, and to encourage. "Praeesse" is an essential obligation. —Aloysius Biskupek, S.V.D.

Because psychoneurosis is due to mental causes, it can be cured only by psychotherapy. —Thomas Vernon Moore, M.D., Carthusian

193.

What will separate us from the love of Christ? Will anguish, or distress, or persecution, or famine, or nakedness, or peril, or the sword? . . . For I am convinced that neither death, nor life, nor angels, nor principalities, nor present things, nor future things, nor powers, nor height, nor depth, nor any other creature will be able to separate us from the love of God in Christ Jesus our Lord. —Romans 8:35, 38, 39

My brother,

The above list of terrible enemies is not, historically, the dangers that separate consecrated priests from Christ. Over all of the centuries, the vast majority of priests have stood up very well under persecution. Many perished as martyrs. Many more endured suffering with great heroism.

No, rather than separate us from Jesus, hardship is more apt to make us willing to share the passion of Christ.

It is, rather, the soft things, the ordinary everyday humdrum events of our daily lives, that wear us down. We become more complacent. The fire of devotion cools. We become more passive. We operate routinely.

Soon we are performing our roles as a priest perfunctorily, without enthusiasm. It is now that a pleasing alternative to Christ can lure us away. Yes, it is often in the ordinary routine of life that our tempter lurks to lead us away from God—from peace.

> Your decrees are my heritage forever;
> they are the joy of my heart. —Psalms 119:111

> Safeguard order and order will safeguard you.
> —St. Augustine

> The priest in order to worthily honor Jesus Christ in the sacrament of the altar, will lead a blameless, pure, and innocent life. —Jacques Millet, S.J.

When I think of all the hours I have spent at Your holy altar, or reciting Your Church's official prayer in my Breviary, then it becomes clear to me that I myself am responsible for making my life so humdrum. . . . O God, it seems we can lose sight of You in anything we do. —Karl Rahner, S.J.

Because of increased bureaucracy, activism is a real danger for the priest today. —Thomas J. McGovern

194.

If anyone does not love the Lord, let him be accursed. Maranatha. —1 Corinthians 16:22

My brother,

In our circle of priestly friends, there are none that do not love the Lord. Yes, they may grow cold. They may find themselves entrapped in situations beyond their control. But not to love the Lord is well nigh impossible.

Too much has passed between God and ourselves to ever cut our relationship. Memory alone, of prayer and solitude, of gentle movements of the soul, of special hours spent in the presence of the Eucharist. All of this and more has created a backdrop that influences our whole life.

Yes, we pray, "Oh, Lord, come!" But it is not the *parousia* that we yearn for. Nor do we seek physical death. No, our prayer, "Oh, Lord, come!" is a call for an ineffable presence—the sweet, cool realization of God within us. Yes, come, Lord—fill our souls with your love. Let us realize that you are here.

It is a strange thing, but at times, the more we seek God, the less present he seems to be. And yet we cannot judge because we are not able to see things objectively.

How many times has a priest presided at a liturgy, climbed a pulpit, and gone through the entire liturgy as if it were someone else performing? It is as if we were operating on remote control.

Yet, how many times has the Lord used our lackluster performance to move souls?

Let your love come to me, LORD,
salvation in accord with your promise. —Psalms 119:41

Silence is a gift from God to let us speak more intently with God. —St. Vincent

It is in solitude that the soul makes progress and penetrates the secrets of the scriptures. In solitude, the soul finds a fountain of tears and purifies itself.
—Thomas à Kempis

The Gospel preached by the church is not just a message, but a divine and life-giving experience for those who believe, hear and obey the message.
—The Priest and the Third Christian Millennium

195.

So give proof before the churches of your love and of our boasting about you to them. —2 Corinthians 8:24

My brother,
Saint Paul is giving us a very tall order, a difficult assignment. "Go ahead," he says, "Show the world your holiness."

How can you do that? All the good works in the world are not necessarily going to be proof of your love. It is merely the result of your inward disposition. Men can read our actions in a multitude of ways—many of them not at all correct.

Show off your love? How does one do that? It takes a lifetime of service to God and man before love is manifest in our lives.

So, just do what you do. Be yourself. Never try to be more than you are. When you are real, all people will sense it. And if they don't read your life properly; well, does it matter?

Goodness will always prove itself. It just takes a little time.

You are the light of the world. . . . Just so, your light must shine before others that they may see your good deeds and glorify your heavenly Father.
—Matthew 5:14–16

He who has the Holy Spirit can be said not only to belong to Christ but to have Christ. For the Spirit cannot be present without Christ also being present. Wherever the hypostatic Trinity is present, the whole Trinity is present. —St. John Chrysostom

Try to do everything in a way that your heart remains free, open, and unchanged. —Devotio Moderna

Every vocation to the priesthood has an individual history of its own. —Pope John Paul II

Even if I were to be Pope, even if my name were to be invoked by all and inscribed on marble monuments, I should still have to stand before the divine judge, and what would I be worth then? Not much.
—Pope John XXIII, as a seminarian

196.

And this is my prayer: that your love may increase ever more and more in knowledge and every kind of perception. . . .
—Philippians 1:9

My brother,
Love is expansive of itself. That is why God made the world. It is why he deigned to call you to share in the priesthood.

So, since love is by nature effusive, your love will pour out and you will abound in holy works.

Understanding is the fruit of wisdom exercised over many years. By seeking truth and wisdom, we nourish our power of judgment. Experience over a long period of time will, if it is properly contemplated, call forth the instinct and keen judgment that we call Wisdom.

Yes, Wisdom is a treasure beyond price. She is like the fine pearl for which we should sell everything else. For true wisdom is nothing less than the Incarnate Word—the Logos—who will transform our lives. Because, if we possess God's wisdom, his Logos, the whole of creation is revealed to us. We see all things clearly and understand all things perfectly.

> But you have the anointing that comes from the holy one, and you all have knowledge. —1 John 2:20

> The Holiness of Jesus is ontological in nature. It is a state that exists prior to activity. —Jean Galot, S.J.

> It is for the priest to learn what is going on among others and in himself in order to carry out an effective mediation for his age. —Gustav Thils

> Ordination fashions a new being. —Jean Galot, S.J.

> I can only stand helpless and feeble before the ultimate mystery of myself, a mystery which lies buried, immovable and unapproachable, in depths beyond the reach of my ordinary freedom. —Karl Rahner, S.J.

> The roar of the world is in my ears
> Thank God for the roar of the world.
> Thank God for the mighty tide of fears
> Against me always hurled.
> Thank God for the bitter and endless strife
> And the sting of his chastening rod.
> Thank God for the stress and pain of life
> And, oh, thank God for God.
> —Joyce Kilmer

BIBLIOGRAPHY

About Being a Priest. Frederico Suarez (Houston: Lumen Christi Press, 1979).

The Diocesan Priest. Gustav Thils (Notre Dame, IN: Fides, 1964).

Encounters with Silence. Karl Rahner, S.J. (South Bend, IN: Saint Augustine's Press, 1999).

The First Five Years of the Priesthood, Dean R. Hoge (Collegeville, MN: The Liturgical Press, 2002).

Jesus Living in the Priest. Jacques Millet, S.J. (New York: Benziger Brothers, 1901).

Journey of a Soul. Pope John XXIII (New York: Signet Books, 1966).

The Postconciliar Priest, Raymond A. Tartre, S.S.S. (New York: P.J. Kenedy & Sons, 1966).

The Priest and the Third Christian Millennium. Congregation for the Clergy (Washington, DC: United States Catholic Conference, 1999).

Priesthood—Conferences on the Rite of Ordination. Aloysius Biskupek, S.V.D. (St. Louis: Herder, 1946).

The Priest in the Third Millennium. Timothy Dolan (Huntington, IN: Our Sunday Visitor Publishing Division, 2000).

Quickening the Fire in Our Midst, George A. Aschenbrenner, S.J. (Chicago: Loyola Press, 2002).

The Report of the Bishops' Ad Hoc Committee for Priestly Life and Ministry—Authority, Maturity, Ministry, Scholarship (Washington, D.C.: United States Catholic Conference Publications Office, 1974).

The Spiritual Life of the Priest. M. Eugene Boylan, O.C.R. (Westminster, MD: Newman Press, 1950).

Theology of the Priesthood. Jean Galot, S.J. (San Francisco: Ignatius Press, 1985).

To All the Bishops of the Church and to All the Priests of the Church. Pope John Paul II.

During his forty-seven years of ministry, Msgr. John J. Gilchrist has been a parish priest, high school teacher, and chaplain. Currently, in addition to his role as pastor of Holy Cross parish in Harrison, New Jersey, Msgr. Gilchrist is a columnist for *The Catholic Advocate*, the Catholic newspaper for the Archdiocese of Newark. He also serves as a liaison to labor for the Archdiocese of Newark. Msgr. Gilchrist was the chairperson of the Newark Archdiocesan Commission for Inter-Religious Affairs.

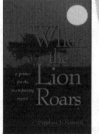